Here is R. T. Kendall at his best.
—DAVE POPE

I would not be surprised if this book becomes a classic.
—GRAHAM KENDRICK

I love this book—full of the Holy Spirit
from a man who loves the Bible.
—SANDY MILLAR

WORSHIPPING GOD

R.T. KENDALL

CHARISMA
HOUSE

Most CHARISMA HOUSE BOOK GROUP products are available at special
quantity discounts for bulk purchase for sales promotions, premiums, fund-
raising, and educational needs. For details, write Charisma House Book
Group, 600 Rinehart Road, Lake Mary, Florida 32746, or telephone (407)
333-0600.

WORSHIPPING GOD by R. T. Kendall
Published by CHARISMA HOUSE
Charisma Media/Charisma House Book Group
600 Rinehart Road
Lake Mary, Florida 32746
www.charismahouse.com

Cover design by Vincent Pirozzi
Design Director: Justin Evans

Visit the author's website at rtkendallministries.com

Library of Congress Cataloging-in-Publication Data:
An application to register this book for cataloging has been submitted to
the Library of Congress.
International Standard Book Number: 978-1-62998-761-3
E-book ISBN: 978-1-62998-762-0

While the author has made every effort to provide accurate Internet
addresses at the time of publication, neither the publisher nor the author
assumes any responsibility for errors or for changes that occur after
publication.

This book was previously published as *Worshipping God* by Hodder &
Stoughton, ISBN 0-340-86332-3, copyright © 1989.

17 18 19 20 21 — 987654321
Printed in the United States of America

To Meint and Linda
Brad, Brent, and Bryce

CONTENTS

Foreword *by Darlene Zschech* ix

Foreword *by Matt Redman* x

Preface xiii

Introduction xv

1   Spirit-Filled Worship 1

2   Empty Form or True Worship 9

3   Honoring the Spirit 16

4   Fellowship 24

5   Worship, Preaching, and the Preacher 29

6   Worship and Listening 36

7   Expectancy 45

8   Worshipping in the Dark 53

9   Worship at the Lord's Table 62

10   The Church at Prayer 70

11   Lifestyle Worship 77

12   Spiritual Gifts and Worship 84

13   Leadership in Worship 92

14   Learning From Angels 97

15   Spiritual Warfare in Worship 106

16   ...With Giving 114

17   ...With Fasting 122

18   ...With Singing 130

19   ...With Music 136

20   ...With the Whole Personality 143

21   Worship and Tradition 153

22   Worship and Liturgy 162

23   The Joy of Doing Nothing 170

24   Worship and Revival 180

25   Preparation for Ultimate Worship 188

26   Worship in Heaven 195

Notes 201

FOREWORD

ABOUT TWELVE MONTHS ago I found myself reading this book, *Worshipping God*, loving the content, loving the challenge, and loving the truths from the Word that were revealed within its pages. I wondered about its author and hoped one day we'd meet. The next day I went to my office and found a fax from R. T. Kendall inviting me to minister at Westminster Chapel in London!

Coincidence, you may say, but I believe God orchestrates these moments for *His* purposes, which one day we may see revealed.

I have seen RT's heart for the local church and his revelation on the power of worship affecting many lives. I really believe that God is restoring worship to *His* church all over the world, *in spirit and in truth.*

The spiritual temperature is certainly heating up and I've heard of and been to hundreds of churches worldwide that say: "We were never a worshipping church, but the hunger for more of Christ has caused us to become one."

Gone are the days of just singing a couple of songs while the late people walk in, or going through the motions of singing some of our old favorites. God is causing His church to *worship* Him with our lives—living a lifestyle of love, and lifting our hearts and voices together in song, experiencing depth and heights in the presence of our precious Lord like never before. There is a wave of praise and worship coming—a new sound, a new song, a unified sound as the church comes together to bless our magnificent Lord.

So, all of you who live to draw closer to our Lord, who love to worship Him: *enjoy this book!*

Let it speak to your heart.

—DARLENE ZSCHECH
HILLSONG CHURCH, NEW SOUTH WALES, AUSTRALIA

FOREWORD

MUSIC IS SUCH a special part of God's blessing in this world. We hear beautiful notes, strains, rhythms, and harmonies that inspire our hearts and offer us further evidence of the Creator. But when we worship God together in song, something beyond even this can occur—a dynamic quite unlike anything else on the earth, outside of the singing, worshipping church. We become the people of God, in the presence of God, pouring out the praises of God.

Yet when it comes to the subject of worship, music is always just the tip of the iceberg. As profound and special as it can be, our musical expressions will never be enough in and of themselves. They must always be backed up by a life of worship. Worship music can help usher us into such a powerful moment, but the call then becomes to complete the integrity of what we have sung with our lives laid down in obedient devotion. In true worship our deeds always outrun our words, and our lives always outweigh our songs.

We see this pattern of worship in Psalm 95. We start out with a call to enter into music and song, and be joyful before God: "O come, let us sing unto the LORD" (v. 1). Next comes the invitation to a posture of reverence and surrender: "O come, let us worship and bow down" (v. 6). But the psalmist lets us know that the journey is by no means complete at that point, for we're told, "Today if you hear His voice, do not harden your hearts" (vv. 7–8). In other words, worship means life change. It means bending your will to the will of the Almighty, submitting your heart, soul, and strength before Him, and conforming more to the likeness of Jesus day by day. As someone once said, "Worship without change is just a game." Hundreds of years earlier, Augustine was thinking along the same lines when he commented on Psalm 149:

Sing to the Lord a new song. "Well I am singing," you say. Yes, you are singing, of course, you are singing, I can hear you. But don't let your life give evidence against your tongue. Sing with your voices, sing also with your hearts; sing with your mouths, sing also with your conduct.[1]

Augustine knew that the song God loves most of all is the one that is not merely found on our lips, but is echoed by our thoughts, words, and deeds.

R. T. Kendall knows the same thing too. What I love about this book is that he gives us the big picture of what worship is. Brilliantly, and pointedly, the chapters on music and singing appear relatively late. Before that we are taught on worship as welcome, witness, word, walk, and warfare. RT shows us on so many different levels, and from so many different angles, what worship is (and what it isn't). We're also reminded that not only is worship a way of life, but it is an eternal activity. I always feel that the very best worship leaders address the everyday while also announcing the eternal. My friend RT does the same in this book—teaching on worship in the day to day, here and now... and worship in the by and by, there and then.

This is an important book. As well as reminding us that worship means the whole of life, Dr. Kendall also speaks into the current worship music movement. In recent years there has been an explosion of new and exciting worship music around the world. With all the good in that, we're also presented with many challenges too. It's essential in these days to shape our view of worship by Scripture and for worship to be as deep, reverent, and Christ-honoring as possible. We are to guard against an emphasis on emotionalism, which can so easily creep in to fill the gaps of weak theology. We are also to guard against entertainment in our worship music, which can so easily creep in because our culture is so heavily infused with it. Though written several years ago, this book remains hugely relevant, and there are some vital warnings and questions inside for musical worship leaders all around the globe. I know I myself felt challenged as I read these pages.

Ultimately, Dr. R. T. Kendall reminds us of the words of Jesus, who taught us that true worship happens in spirit and in truth. May God use this brilliant book to make better worshippers of us all.

—MATT REDMAN

PREFACE

I AM NOT AN expert on the subject of worship. I never dreamed that I would write a book on this subject.

What happened was this. I began preaching from Philippians in January 1985. During the autumn of 1986, when we were still using the Authorized Version, we reached Philippians 3:3: "We are the circumcision who worship God in the Spirit." I planned to preach a sermon on worship. In translating the Greek, I found that Paul actually said, "We worship by the Spirit of God," that is, by the impulse of the Spirit.

I felt that a second sermon was needed. But when I finished it, various members of the congregation urged me to go on with this subject. I agreed to a third sermon. I was not prepared for the excitement I myself felt, and I think others felt as well. I kept going and the series exceeded the number of chapters of this book.

In 1995 Paul Cain preached a sermon on the subject of worship that was epoch-making. It did more to change our church generally and my own life particularly than any other sermon I have listened to in years and years. The funny thing is this book was written *before* Paul Cain came to us. His influence on us in this area only accentuated all I said. Nothing I wrote needed changing; I can only say I believe all I wrote then twice as much now!

A host of friends have kindly commended this book, and I thank them most warmly. I am especially thankful to Darlene Zschech for her foreword. I had to pinch myself on a memorable Sunday evening in May 1998 when she led us in worship at Westminster, singing "Shout to the Lord"; it seemed too good to be true. It showed how far the chapel has come since I wrote this book, and yet how the exposition of God's unchanging Word remains the same.

Since the first edition of this book came out, I have had the privilege of meeting Matt Redman. He has become a great friend and has kindly written another foreword for this new edition of Worshipping God. He is one of the great song-writers and worship leaders of our generation. His song "Ten Thousand Reasons" has matched Darlene's "Shout to the Lord."

When I first began bonefishing on Largo Sound in 1964, I could not have known that one day my family and I would be offered the use of a home right on that tropical paradise. Captain and Mrs. Meint Huesman began turning their home, boat, and car over to us in 1984. I gratefully and affectionately dedicate this volume to them and their three sons.

In the meantime I have improved my bonefishing skills. But one of my greatest thrills was to lead Don Gurgiolo to Christ in the summer of 1982 (see introduction). I can also now regard a number of professional bonefish guides as friend! Jack Brothers (now in heaven), Harry Spear, Oz Keagy, and John Sutter have repeatedly taken me fishing in exchange for my teaching them more about the Bible as we fish—and worship—together.

—R. T. KENDALL
LONDON
FEBRUARY 1999

INTRODUCTION

THERE IS AN old story about two churches in Alabama—one Baptist, the other Methodist—that were located across the street from each other. Both were holding a "revival" at the same time. Sadly a rivalry had developed between the two churches over the years, partly due to theological differences. Later some Baptists were heard to comment, "Well, we didn't have much of a revival, but thank God the Methodists didn't either."

In America the word *revival* is used hastily and uncritically to describe what, in Britain, we prefer to call a mission. *Revival*, strictly speaking, is indeed too often the wrong word, particularly when authentic revival doesn't come. But it is not surprising that real revival doesn't come when there is such a rivalry and competitive spirit as I just described. The Holy Spirit is surely grieved.

But I suspect that the British too have their Achilles' heel when it comes to the use of a word: *worship*. How often have I heard the phrase, "We are going to have a time of worship," when all that really happens is a time of singing hymns or choruses. I fear that worship no more takes place than revival does! And yet it is not surprising that real worship doesn't take place, and that is why I have written this book.

Worship is only really done by the Holy Spirit. As genuine revival only comes by the Holy Spirit, so too does true worship. The Holy Spirit is as essential to one as the other.

To illustrate this crucial point, let me share my favorite sermon illustration with you. My hobby is bonefishing. A man once came into my vestry and asked, "What is bonefishing?" Jokingly I replied, "It is a requirement for membership of Westminster Chapel!"

Bonefishing is a shallow water sport that is done in the

tropical, clear waters of the sea. The only place it is found in the United States is in the Florida Keys, a string of small islands between Miami and Key West. The bonefish (so named because it is full of bones and largely inedible) is a wily, skittish but very powerful fish, caught with a rod and reel, averaging between five and ten pounds. It is usually caught by simultaneous hunting and fishing. You literally stalk them in inches of water near the shorelines. The ideal depth of water is between the ankle and knee. One of the best ways to catch them is to wade for them, providing you do so discreetly and quietly. For if they see you before you see them, they explode in nervous fear and take off like a discharged torpedo. By then it is too late to catch them. One usually needs a professional guide to locate and catch them. A real sportsman moreover releases all his fish unharmed.

I had heard a lot about bonefishing, especially when my wife and I would travel to the Keys for other kinds of fishing. The more I heard and read about bonefishing, the more I wanted to give it a try. It began in 1964. I decided to rent a boat at Gilbert's Fishing Camp at Jewfish Creek, just north of Key Largo. I said to the manager, "I want to go bonefishing."

He said, "Fine, who is your guide?"

"I don't need a guide."

"Are you a bonefisherman?"

"I will be after today."

"Have you ever been bonefishing before?"

"No."

"Nobody—nobody but a fool—goes bonefishing without a guide," the manager warned me.

"Will you please rent me a boat?" I asked.

"Sure, I'll rent you a boat."

"Will you show me on the map where to go?"

He obliged. "Go out across Blackwater Sound, then go through this small cut that takes you into Largo Sound. On the other side of the shoreline there are plenty of bonefish." I had my rod and reel and plenty of live shrimp for bait. I went out about ten o'clock in the morning.

When I returned, just before sundown, the fishing camp manager asked, "How many did you catch?"

"There weren't any," I replied with no little chagrin.

"Go look over there and look in that ice chest," he said.

In that chest was a huge, ten-pound bonefish that someone had caught earlier that day. It was waiting to be collected by a taxidermist, for a lot of people pay to have their first bonefish mounted as a trophy to remind them of their proud accomplishment. It almost made me sick with envy. "Where was that fish caught?" I asked.

"Largo Sound," came the reply.

The man who actually caught that big bonefish overheard us talking. He said to me, "We saw you in Largo Sound. There were bonefish all over the place. Didn't you see them?"

The camp manager laughed. "I told you that you should have a guide."

Never in my life was I so frustrated, not to say humbled. I did not hire a professional guide because I didn't want to pay their fee and I wanted particularly to demonstrate that I was such an exceptional fisherman that I could bring in a bonefish all by myself without the help of a guide.

I refused to give in. I read all the articles on bonefishing from fishing magazines I could get my hands on. I returned to the same place the following week, fully prepared to catch my first bonefish without the assistance of a guide.

But it was a repeat performance. So was the week after that. I am too embarrassed to tell you how many weeks—and months—I went to Largo Sound, only to return at the end of the day without catching, or even seeing, my first bonefish. I spent far more money on boat rentals than the professional guide would have cost. And my pride had been dealt with as well.

I finally gave in. "Find me the best guide in the Keys," I ordered.

"The man you want is Don Gurgiolo."

I phoned him and booked him. "Where do I meet you?" I asked.

"Largo Sound," came the reply.

I was disappointed. I wanted to go where there were bonefish. But we headed straight across to the other side of Largo Sound. "There are no fish here," I said unwisely. He turned off the motor and began poling the boat. (I experienced the nearest equivalent to poling when I took my family punting on the Cherwell in Oxford.)

"Shh, look over there—eighty feet at ten o'clock (the bow of the boat being twelve)—a nine pound bonefish," Don whispered with excitement after only five minutes.

"Where? I don't see anything."

"It's too late now, he's gone. Don't worry, there'll be another."

There was, but I missed him too.

"Relax, Kendall. Do you see that white spot at two o'clock? Keep your eyes on that spot. The fish isn't there yet, he's at twelve o'clock, two hundred feet away. He's coming toward one. Now he's at two o'clock. See him?"

I did. "So that's a bonefish!" I muttered. Before the day was over I was able to see them. We actually hooked five by the time we had to return to the dock.

What made the difference? The guide.

Jesus said of the Holy Spirit, "He will guide you into all truth" (John 16:13). Without the Spirit's help we cannot grasp spiritual truth. "The natural man does not receive the things of the Spirit of God," said Paul, "for they are foolishness to him; nor can he know them, because they are spiritually discerned" (1 Cor. 2:14). We may think we can grasp the Bible and the things of the Spirit without the Spirit, but such thinking is utter folly. The truth is there, but we will not see it or grasp it until we humbly depend on the Spirit to help us.

So too with worshipping God.

CHAPTER 1

SPIRIT-FILLED WORSHIP

For we are the circumcision who worship
God in the Spirit, and boast in Christ
Jesus, and place no trust in the flesh.

—PHILIPPIANS 3:3

I BELIEVE THAT EVERY Christian has one fundamental calling and one primary duty—a duty which is also a delight. We are called, by the way we live and in all we do, to worship God. This is a full-time activity, not only here on earth, but in heaven too.

Every church, therefore, must ask one basic question: How can our services lead the people out in a spirit of worship? A church should not be preoccupied with perpetuating a certain tradition or be looking over its shoulder to see what others are doing. Instead, it should be asking, "How do we conduct services that are honoring to God?" This is the important thing, no matter who may be offended as a result.

But what exactly is worship? How do we worship God? What is involved? In Philippians 3:3 Paul says that we "worship God in the Spirit," or—as the ESV translates it—"by the Spirit of God." (The Greek means those "who serve under the impulse of the Spirit of God.") I believe that the key to understanding and experiencing worship lies in this verse. True worship is in the Spirit or by the Spirit of God.

Two Greek words in the New Testament are translated by our word *worship.* One is *proskuneo,* which is used sixty times and means "to adore, to give reverence to."[1] This refers to the condition of the heart. It is the word used by Jesus when he said to the woman of Samaria, "God is Spirit, and those who worship Him must worship Him in spirit and in truth" (John 4:24).

The other word is *latreuontes*, which appears as a noun or a verb twenty-one times, and may be translated as "service."[2] This is the word which is used to refer to public worship, and comes in Philippians 3:3: "…who worship [serve] God in the Spirit." Thus both words are used in the context of Spirit-led and Spirit-controlled worship.

In this first chapter I want to give a definition of *worship* and show what the design, or aim, of worship is. I then want to deal with doubtful worship and finally give a description of dynamic worship.

Here, then, is my own definition of *worship*: it is "the response to, and/or preparation for, the preached Word." I say this, not because I am trying to defend the Reformed tradition, or because I want to perpetuate any church's tradition as a preaching center, but because I happen to be convinced that worship as described in the New Testament makes preaching central.

I think everyone would agree that the greatest service that has ever been held took place on the Day of Pentecost. Acts 2:42 gives us a description of the pattern of the earliest known Christian worship. We read: "They continued steadfastly in the apostles' teaching and fellowship, in the breaking of bread and in the prayers." This was obviously in response to the preached Word.

What, then, is the role of the Spirit in worship? As we have seen, in John 4:24 Jesus said, "God is Spirit, and those who worship Him must worship Him in spirit and truth." The Spirit always comes first. In worship the Spirit prepares our minds and hearts to receive God's Word, and, as we see at Pentecost, it is the Spirit who brings about a change of heart and enables us to continue in the apostles' doctrine.

Incidentally, some people set great store by the building in which they worship. Perhaps the woman of Samaria was one of these, for she said, "Our fathers worshipped on this mountain" (John 4:20). But when Jesus said, "God is Spirit, and those who worship Him must worship Him in spirit and truth," He was telling us that the place and building are not important.

But if the first thing is the Spirit, what is the role of the truth? Truth—Christian doctrine as revealed in the Word of God—is the proof and guarantee that one is in the Spirit; it also serves as a yardstick for testing actions which are allegedly in the Spirit but which in fact are not. The truth keeps worship from going off the rails. The Bible was not given to replace the Holy Spirit The Bible is there to correct abuse, and to help us make sure that our worship and our Christian walk are genuinely in the Spirit.

The object of our worship is, of course, the triune God. Look again at Philippians 3:3: "We...worship God in the Spirit, and boast in Christ Jesus." Worship centers on God, with special attention given to praising God for Jesus—for who He is and what He has done.

A. W. Tozer, in his book *Whatever Happened to Worship?*, cites Dr. George D. Watson, who said there are two levels in the worship of God: gratitude and excellence. He went on to say that most people never get beyond the level of gratitude; few worship God for His excellence, for all that He is, for His transcendent and immanent glory.[3]

When we think of God's transcendence, we usually think of the glory of God. Many of our hymns praise God for His majesty, His glory, and His awe-inspiring throne. And to some people, this aspect of God is all that matters. But there is another side to the worship of God. Paul said, "And because you are sons, God has sent forth into our hearts the Spirit of His Son, crying, 'Abba, Father!'" (Gal. 4:6). And in Romans 8:16 Paul said, "The Spirit Himself bears witness with our spirits that we are the children of God." This is the most intimate language. "Abba, Father" literally means (I almost blush to use it)—"Daddy."

Many of us are so sophisticated that the only kind of worship we can envisage is that which deals with the transcendence of God, and we are offended by some of the more intimate choruses. But we need to realize that it is just as honoring to God to praise Him for His immanence as it is to praise Him for His transcendence. By God's immanence, I mean the wonderful way He works within nature, within our world and daily events, and deep within our lives. I mean His closeness to us. One Sunday someone came to me and said, "Dr. Kendall, I want to share something with you. I was praying recently and I felt that God was asking me to put my arms around Him. So I did—I just stood up and put my arms around the Lord. And the warmest feeling came over me." Now that story may offend some people, but it didn't offend me.

This leads me on to look at the aim of our worship. Our aim should be to glorify God and edify the soul of every person present. It's easy to talk about glorifying God, but what does it mean? Someone may say, "It's being sound in your doctrine and singing hymns about God's glory." But that is too superficial an answer. To glorify God means to please Him. We must continually ask ourselves this very searching question: When we meet together to worship God, is it our aim to please Him or to please ourselves?

I know that the answer here can be "both," and in the end that is true. But we will never succeed in pleasing God until we forget about ourselves. There is a parallel here with buying presents. There are two ways of buying presents. We can think, "Oh, I've got to buy so-and-so a present or they'll wonder why I didn't." And we just buy any old thing. Or we can take our time because we want to get a present which will thrill the recipient. We don't just choose something that we would like to be given, but we buy what we hope will give pleasure to the other person. For the joy of giving is in making someone else happy.

And it is the same with worship. We want to bring joy to God. There is, however, one crucial difference between giving presents to our friends and offering worship to God: it is not for us to try to decide what will please God. God has already decided what kind of worship He wants. Worship that pleases Him must be "by the Spirit of God."

"Well," someone may say, "if I'm going to worship God by His Spirit, then I'm not really doing anything. It's just God doing it for Himself. But I want to please Him by showing Him what I can do." But anyone who talks like this does not know God because God doesn't want what we can do. He has already decided what He wants, and we must decide whether we are going to worship in His way. As the writer to the Hebrews says, "Through Him, then, let us continually offer to God the sacrifice of praise" (Heb. 13:15). The word *sacrifice* is used here because to worship by the Spirit of God involves self-denial. It is a *sacrifice* of praise.

One of the earliest worship services in the history of mankind is described in Genesis 4. And in it Cain decided that he would worship God by bringing an offering of the works of his own hands, while his brother, Abel, sacrificed some of his best lambs. But God wanted a sacrifice. So "the LORD had respect for Abel and for his offering, but for Cain and for his offering, He did not have respect" (vv. 4–5).

Our aim in worship must be to please God, but the aim of worship is also to edify the soul of every person present. The key word here is *every* person. God is worshipped not just when we do certain things right, but when we are edified— that is, when our spirits are fed with His Word so that we reach out to Him in repentance, gratitude, and trust. He is glorified when we worship Him with our understanding, not when we intone, parrot-fashion, words like "Majestic sweetness sits enthroned..."[4] And He is not fully glorified if only some people are edified.

If we are rigid in our services, only a limited number of people will be blessed. If the order of worship is controlled by those who say, "We've always done it this way," then our worship may be irrelevant to new people. Why aren't we reaching out to the world? The answer may be that much of our worship is irrelevant. Why are some Anglo-Catholic churches dying?

It's not just because of their literal theology, but because their worship doesn't speak to people where they are. Only a minority of people today are interested in burning incense. And evangelical churches, with their rigid traditions, may also be failing to reach people. So often they are too busy arguing about minor points of order to get on with the task of evangelism.

A few years ago an academic study looked at revival in the third world to see if the different revivals had any factors in common. Revivals in countries like South Korea and in cities like Nairobi were studied. The conclusion was that they all had five things in common: an emphasis first, on prayer; second, on evangelism; third, on discipleship; fourth, on one church for all the people in the area; and fifth, on relevant worship.

Psychological studies tell us that a truly mature person is one who is adaptable. A refusal to accept the new and different may not indicate godliness or spiritual maturity, but fear. If our worship is to glorify God by being relevant, we must be willing to accept changes. There must be something for all types of people in our services. I believe that when revival comes, we will not find just one class of people in our churches, but all types and groups.

But I turn now to my third point, and that is doubtful worship. Philippians 3:3 says, "We...boast in Christ Jesus, and place no trust in the flesh." I am talking here about worship that is "fleshly," worship that is not dependent on God's Spirit. Such worship has three characteristics, the first of which is emotionalism. I can give you an example of this. I was once in Ohio, preaching for Dr. Billy Ball. As we were driving down Interstate 75 on our way back to the airport, we saw in the distance the old Union Station in Cincinnati, and I asked if we would have time to stop there. When I was a boy, my mother and I used to visit her parents in Illinois, and on the way we would always change trains in Cincinnati. We usually had an hour to spare, and I would walk all over this big station—the largest in the world at that time, and said to be the most beautiful. Today it's a shopping center because the railway industry in America has declined.

So we stopped, and I walked around the building with tears in my eyes. When I got back in the car, I said, "You'll never know what that did for me!" It had made me feel so good to be there. But the experience was emotional rather than spiritual.

And this sort of thing can happen in worship. We may like the building, the sound of the organ, or the tunes of the hymns; we may feel good when we hear, "A mighty fortress is our God,"[5] or—as we used to sing back in the hills of Kentucky—"Tell Mother I'll be there, in answer to her prayer."[6] But our "good" feelings may be emotional only. May God grant us objectivity about ourselves, so that we can analyze why we are moved and ask, "Is it truly of the Spirit or just a natural human emotion?"

Another characteristic of fleshly, doubtful worship is elitism, that is, worship that favors one cultural group and excludes others. For example, I love the pipe organ; in Westminster Chapel we have one of the finest organs in the country. But it is elitist to have only organ music in church.

A third characteristic is that it is entertainment worship, or worship that is for people's pleasure. Any worship that seeks to amuse or entertain people is only a performance and is to be despised. God wants us to use our talents, but for His glory. Godly singers and musicians lead us out to focus on God and worship Him. When we find we are concentrating on the performer and praising him or her—that is fleshly, entertainment worship.

So, finally, I would like to describe dynamic worship. The word *dynamic* means "fluid, moving." It is the opposite of static. Jonathan Edwards taught us that the task of every generation is to discover in which direction the sovereign Redeemer is moving, and then to move in that direction.

Dynamic worship is worship by the Spirit of God. And we will know that the Spirit is present in our worship if these three things follow: an increase of faith, an increase of fellowship, and an increase of freedom. We will leave after a service

7

feeling we have faith to face a thousand worlds, with love in our hearts towards every single person in the church, and without our dreadful feelings of self-consciousness, for "where the Spirit of the Lord is, there is liberty" (2 Cor. 3:17).

A telling sign of true revival is that people are oblivious of everything but God. A couple of years ago I spoke to a man who had experienced revival in Africa. When I asked him to tell me about it, he said, "Nobody was self-conscious. You were conscious only of God." This means that we will not be intimidated by others. In his book *Whatever Happened to Worship?* A. W. Tozer has this to say about Jesus's words, "I tell you, if these should be silent, the stones would immediately cry out" (Luke 19:40):

> Let me say two things here.
>
> First, I do not believe it is necessarily true that we are worshipping God when we are making a lot of racket. But not infrequently worship is audible.
>
> When Jesus came into Jerusalem presenting himself as Messiah, there was a great multitude, and there was a great noise. Doubtless many who joined in the singing and the praise had never been able to sing in the right key. When you have a group of people singing anywhere, you know that some of them will not be in tune. But this is the point to their worship: they were united in praises to God.
>
> Second, I would warn those who are cultured, quiet, self-possessed, poised and sophisticated, that if they are embarrassed in church when some happy Christian says, "Amen," they may actually be in need of some spiritual enlightenment. The worshipping saints of God in the body of Christ have often been a little bit noisy.[7]

In heaven there will be no sense of pride or of fear; no looking over our shoulder. Heaven will be filled with praise to the "Lamb who is in the midst of the throne" (Rev. 7:17).

CHAPTER 2

EMPTY FORM OR TRUE WORSHIP

For we are the circumcision who worship
God in the Spirit, and boast in Christ
Jesus, and place no trust in the flesh.

—Philippians 3:3

I N CHAPTER 1, I talked about suspect, or counterfeit, worship. Worship that is elitist or is reduced to the level of popular entertainment, worship that is emotional or aesthetic is worship in name only. It has the external form without the reality. What we long for is living worship. But how does this come about?

I think the principle to follow is to be found in Psalm 37:4, "Delight yourself in the LORD, and He will give you the desires of your heart." That is true for all of us, whomever we are or whatever we want. But when we delight ourselves in the Lord, some of our desires may wither away and be replaced by new ambitions. So it will not do to envisage a definite goal concerning the form our worship must take. We must first of all be sure that we are delighting ourselves in the Lord and then see what God does.

I want to show you from Paul's words in Philippians 3:3 that worship that is "by the Spirit of God" has three stages: first, the initiation of the Spirit; second, the impulse of the Spirit; and third, the inheritance of the Spirit.

So, firstly, the *initiation of the Spirit*. We must see here that God's elect—that is, those whom God has chosen—are a people

9

of the Spirit. Now the Jews in Paul's day said that the people of God were those who had been circumcised. To this day, one is officially a Jew if one has a Jewish mother. Being a Jew is either inherited or initiated by circumcision. Many think it is the same with Christianity. They think that to be a Christian you must be born into a Christian home, be baptized, or attend a Christian church.

Not so, says Paul. God's elect are a people of the Spirit. In Romans 9:6–7 Paul says, "For they are not all Israel who are descended from Israel, nor are they all children because they are descendants of Abraham, but 'In Isaac shall your descendants be called.'" Ishmael, though a son of Abraham, was regarded as strictly of the flesh, whereas Isaac was the child of promise, and he was of the Spirit.

When Paul says, "We are the circumcision," he means that God's people are circumcised in the heart: "Circumcision is of the heart" (Rom. 2:29). And this is a sovereign work of the Holy Spirit. Jesus said, "It is the Spirit who gives life. The flesh profits nothing" (John 6:63). And Paul said in Romans 8:2: "For the law of the Spirit of life in Christ Jesus has set me free from the law of sin and death." The only people who truly worship God are the people of the Spirit, who have had this operation of the Holy Spirit upon the foreskins of their hearts. Only the elect can worship God with spiritual worship. All others may say that they worship, but they are worshipping idols.

Our churches should not be places where the unregenerate come on Sundays because they "like the worship." Our churches ought to be places where the unregenerate feel uncomfortable because it is the Spirit who is important and who comes first. Our controlling principle must be obedience to the Spirit—no matter where He leads us.

And, further, worship that is initiated by the Spirit is always of the Spirit, by the Spirit, and in the Spirit. *Of the spirit* refers to those who have been brought to the new birth; *by the Spirit* describes what these reborn people are able to do—they serve God under the impulse of the Spirit. And this is an internal thing, a matter of the heart. It may be expressed externally, but it is immaterial whether this be by tambourine, guitar, or pipe organ.

Lastly, worship that is *in the Spirit* is brought about when, under the impulse of the Spirit, God's people are taken a step further so that they begin to adore the triune God on a level that is different from anything they have ever experienced before, a level which transcends elitist or emotional or entertainment worship. And this is not something which can be worked up by hand-clapping, or forcing your hand into the air, or by any self-induced enthusiasm.

This leads me to my second point: *the impulse of the Spirit*. As I have said, the Greek of Philippians 3:3 reads, "who worship by the impulse of the Spirit." Now this is a very important concept, yet I have a suspicion that we largely do not know anything about it. You have probably heard it said that if the Holy Spirit left a church, ninety percent of the work of that church would go right on as if nothing had happened. And I suspect that this would also be true with reference to church worship.

We say, "Oh, but we like it this way. We have always done it this way." But where does the impulse of the Spirit come in?

In true worship the people of the Spirit are enabled by the Spirit to participate in the worship that God feels for Himself. For God loves Himself—and if we don't like that fact, it is because a God of glory is offensive to our fleshly human nature. God does everything for His own glory, and "works all things according to the counsel of His own will" (Eph. 1:11). And everything in all creation was designed for the worship of God. If you don't like the idea of worshipping God, if you want to go your own way and do your own thing, then you are going against the very reason God made you. God's entire plan of salvation is designed to bring us to the place where we worship God: "Let all the angels of God worship Him" (Heb. 1:6). "Let everything that has breath [whether it be fish or fowl, mammal or flower] praise the LORD" (Ps. 150:6). "The heavens declare the glory of God" (Ps. 19:1). Under the impulse of the Spirit we are brought to worship God as God worships Himself. And therefore, if we are worshipping under the impulse of the Spirit, we ourselves are not doing anything. In John 6:63 we read: "The flesh profits nothing." Paul continues Philippians 3:3 with the words, "Place no trust in the flesh."

As long as we think that we are doing something—that there is something in us, whether it be our talents, our efforts, our self-denial, or an idea that we can make promises to God—and as long as we call this worship, then we need to be reminded that we are taking our cue from the flesh. We need to be advised that this is mainly self-love, not the worship of God.

We must also understand that worship by the impulse of the Spirit is done by degrees. And some may experience a higher degree of this impulse than others. As we have seen, the principle here is that the greater the measure of the Spirit, the less we will be conscious of those around us, and the more we will become aware of God. Should the Spirit increase in us in great measure (what a blessed thought!), the result might be total unconsciousness. John on the Isle of Patmos said, "When I saw Him, I fell at His feet as though I were dead" (Rev. 1:17). The prophet Ezekiel said, "The glory of the God of Israel was there…in the plain…and I fell on my face" (Ezek. 8:4; 9:8).

The Cane Ridge Revival in America has been called America's Second Great Awakening. It is not so well known because there were no great preachers like Edwards or Whitefield. Instead there were provincial preachers. One Sunday morning in August 1801, fifteen thousand people came under the influence of the Spirit, and eyewitnesses said that that Sunday morning service continued without a break until midday on the following Wednesday.

People were praising God and worshipping and as many as five hundred at a time were unconscious on the ground. They were thought to be dead. Their pulses were checked and were found to be down to only two or three beats a minute. And yet the people came out of it with a great sense of God.

That's having a degree of the Spirit!

There is a famous story from the Welsh Revival. A man came home from the coal mines to find that for the fifth or sixth night in succession his wife had gone down to the church where the revival was taking place and had not prepared his supper. He was so mad that he went down to the revival with the express purpose of busting it wide open and pulling his wife out.

But when he got to the church, it was so crowded that he couldn't get in. There were even people standing outside. He tried to work his way through, and the next thing he knew, he was on his knees in front of the altar with his hands in the air, praying.

That measure of the Spirit has happened in church history, but this generation, and that includes those in the charismatic movement, I fear know little or nothing about it.

I would like to give a two-fold warning here. First, never think that an outpouring of the Holy Spirit will convince everybody. And second, never think that those who are affected will be affected equally.

Perhaps the key here is the sovereignty of the Spirit. It is one thing to believe in the sovereignty of the Spirit with reference to salvation, but another to believe in His sovereignty with reference to worship. You may be affected, but the person next to you may be totally unmoved. You may be thinking, "Oh, Lord, this is marvelous," and then you may wonder what is going on in your neighbor's mind. What a pity if you were to grieve or quench the Spirit, or cast aside His impulse, because you were influenced by what another might or might not be thinking.

You may say, "Surely, if the Spirit comes in power, I won't be concerned with anybody else." But it's not always as simple as that. Jesus said, "He who is faithful in what is least is faithful also in much" (Luke 16:10). I used to think that if revival ever came to my own church, Westminster Chapel, I would then be able to get away with calling people forward. And people would say, "There's such power here, they're coming forward in droves."

But then I realized that I had to call people forward in a non-revival atmosphere, painful though that might be. And so with each individual. You may want that great power, but "He who is faithful in what is least is faithful also in much." When you are in a church service, God could pass by the person next to you for the moment, but if you go by what is happening to him and so quench the Spirit in yourself, you will miss the blessing, which may well come to your neighbor later. In fact, God may slay the person next to you later and never come back to you at all because looking over your shoulder all the time shows that you care more about what people think than what God thinks.

The warning is that it is possible to be present where the Spirit is working in great power and yet feel nothing yourself. Never say, "I would know an authentic work of the Spirit," for that kind of pride only grieves the Spirit. God could come in great power and people could be affected, but you might not feel a thing. You might even laugh and say, "Look at them—silly people!"

When Jesus raised Lazarus from the dead, you would think everybody would have believed in Him. But they didn't. We read that, "Therefore many of the Jews who came to Mary, and saw what Jesus had done, believed in Him. But some of them went away to the Pharisees and told them what Jesus had done" (John 11:45–46).

I used to say to myself, "If only revival would come, all those who oppose my ministry would see that I really am a man of God." But Luke 16:10 says, "He who is dishonest in the least is dishonest also in much." No great movement of the Spirit has ever convinced everybody. Have you any idea of the kind of critics Evan Roberts had in his day? Or of the number who criticized Whitefield and Edwards?

I think we would all agree that Stephen, the first deacon, preached with unction. And you couldn't have suggested to the Pharisee, Saul of Tarsus, that he would not recognize the work of God. He considered himself an authority on it. But

Saul of Tarsus heard Stephen preach and was unimpressed. There was Stephen, with his face shining like an angel, saying, "Look! I see the heavens opened and the Son of Man standing at the right hand of God" (Acts 7:56). Yet Saul consented to Stephen's death.

Never think that you are so in touch with God that nothing could come to your church without your knowing it first. One of the errors of some charismatic Christians is that they see the Spirit as a warm blanket that falls on everybody so that everybody feels the same thing. But the outpouring of the sovereign Spirit is essentially upon individuals. Each worshipper is responsible to God alone. The task for each of us is to say, "God, it's You I worship." God is willing to pour out His Spirit on those who look to Him only. Jesus said, "How can you believe, who receive glory from one another and do not seek the glory that comes from the only God?" (John 5:44).

So now I move on to *the inheritance of the Spirit*. This is when the Holy Spirit is utterly Himself in us. When someone comes into our house, we say, "Do make yourself at home." If you really want the Spirit to be at home in you—to be Himself in you—you must open your heart directly to Him and say, "Lord, I do love You, and I will do what You say."

Complete obedience to the Spirit at home within us is the key to true worship, either when we are by ourselves or with other Christians at church. The worship we experience when we are alone ought to be multiplied a hundred times when we come to the church worship service. Otherwise we are godly on weekdays and hypocrites on Sundays. If we say that we are loving and seeking God, but quench the Spirit when we meet together with other Christians, what kind of love is that?

Do we want revival—the culmination of true worship? It's easier to pray twice a day for it than obey God when He says, "But here's what I want you to do." We may admire Evan Roberts, who said in agony, "Lord, bend me." But God is asking all of us to say, "Bend me" and mean it, regardless of the cost.

15

CHAPTER 3

HONORING THE SPIRIT

*For we...worship God in the Spirit, and boast
in Christ Jesus, and place no trust in the flesh.*

—PHILIPPIANS 3:3

I F YOU WERE to ask people to describe to you their idea of a perfect service of worship, I suspect that many, or most, would start by describing the external organization and shape of the service. Should there be banjos or violins or organ music? Should there be a hymnal or choruses? What about the prayer book?

However, as I hope I have shown, I am not primarily concerned with that, although it would be interesting to see what forms of worship would emerge in a church fully given over to the leading of the Spirit.

We have seen that God is a God of glory. He loves Himself and "works all things according to the counsel of His own will" (Eph. 1:11). He knows how He wants to be worshipped; it won't do for us, in our desire for creativity, just to come up with a way we *think* honors Him. We must be controlled by the Spirit from start to finish.

As Paul says, we must "place no trust in the flesh" (Phil. 3:3). If we begin with the form of worship, we are beginning with the flesh because at once we are superimposing a cultural norm on the worship. But how will we ever know what is truly spiritual? How will we avoid "having a form of godliness, but denying its power" (2 Tim. 3:5)?

When I look at Philippians 3:3, the immediate question that

I ask is, "What does it mean to bring the Spirit into our worship?" When Paul says, "We…worship in the Spirit," what does that mean?

In this chapter I want to look at three possible approaches to the Holy Spirit. The first possibility is hiring Him, that is, engaging His services for temporary use. The second is hindering the Spirit—Paul calls it "grieving" Him. And the third is honoring Him.

First, hiring Him. How do we hire the Spirit? The word *hire* means "to engage the services of a person or a place or a thing." I think that many of us in our worship are like someone without a car who wants to take a trip from London to Brighton, and wonders how to get there—by train, perhaps, or by hiring a car.

Suppose we decide to rent a car, a Ford Focus perhaps. We walk up to it and say, "Hmm—looks like a nice car." But do we then say, "How are you doing, Ford Focus? Where would you like to go today?" Of course we don't! We make it do what we want, because it has no will of its own. And many of us do just this with the Holy Spirit. We treat Him as if He has no will of His own. We think of Him as standing idly by, wanting to be used, like a car waiting to be hired.

We decide what we want to include in our services and what our aim is to be and then tell the Holy Spirit to take us there. When we hire the Spirit in this way, we manipulate Him to serve our own ends, and that is a great abuse.

Another abuse of the Spirit that results from hiring Him is to try and work Him up to go our way. I have been in places where there has been fifteen or twenty minutes of clapping and tambourine playing to get the service going. Sometimes you almost feel as though you are watching American cheerleaders before a football game.

We have an instance of this kind of approach in 1 Kings 18, when Elijah challenged the prophets of Baal to meet him on Mount Carmel and see who was worshipping the true God.

> Elijah said to the prophets of Baal, "Choose one bull for yourselves and prepare it first, for there are many of you, and call on the name of your god, but do not light a fire underneath."
>
> They took the bull which was given to them, and they prepared it and called on the name of Baal from morning until noon, saying, "O Baal, hear us." But there was no voice, and no one answered. And they leaped upon the altar which was made.
>
> By noon, Elijah mocked them, saying, "Cry out loud, for he is a god. Either he is talking or is gone away or is on a journey, or perhaps he is asleep and needs to be awakened." They cried out loud and cut themselves with knives and spears according to their custom until the blood gushed out on them.
>
> —1 KINGS 18:25–28

This sort of behavior is merely of the flesh. People suppose that noise proves the presence of the Spirit. I have already quoted the remark by A. W. Tozer that, when the Spirit is powerfully present, there is often a lot of noise, and I agree with that. But Tozer himself also said that noise does not always prove that the Spirit is there.

I come next to hindering the Spirit. One way of doing this is to hem Him around with our own preconceived ideas and prejudices. This happens when we come to worship after having already decided on the form the worship should take. Nothing quenches the Spirit like prejudice of this sort. And one problem is that so often we don't recognize it in ourselves. Whether our prejudices are racial or cultural, intellectual or political, we feel good about them and think they must be right. And because we feel so good, because we feel at home with our prejudices, we think that what we are feeling comes from the Holy Spirit. It is a subtle trap. And as a result many people never have any idea of what God can do in them and through them.

It is wrong to claim that a particular form, which was once truly used by the Spirit, must therefore always be the only valid form. The Welsh Revival, for example, was often criticized because its emphasis was on singing and there was so little preaching, for in the days of Whitefield preaching had the priority.

The question for us is: Where is God now? The Spirit is not for hire. We don't have to work anything up, for the Spirit has a will of His own, and He alone knows what the God of glory desires. Our task is to listen to Him and find out what this is.

Another way of hindering the Spirit is to shut Him out by our hardness of heart. Sometimes we have a proud, independent attitude that the Spirit just cannot penetrate.

You may say, "But God is sovereign. He can work by irresistible grace." It is true that this applies sooner or later in the effectual calling of the elect, but it does not apply to the living of the Christian life. The doctrine of sanctification is *not* worked out by irresistible grace. If our sanctification happened automatically, through irresistible grace, we would not need the New Testament or the urgings of Paul.

The fact is that the Holy Spirit, although He works effectually in bringing people to saving faith, is easily grieved and hindered, and when we come to church with hard hearts, nothing will happen. Maybe we do not physically have our arms folded, but we do in spirit; maybe we are not outwardly stiff-necked, but we are in spirit. We justify our pride and our failure to love, and think all this has nothing to do with worship. But remember that Jesus said, "You are those who justify yourselves before men, but God knows your hearts. For that which is highly esteemed before men is an abomination before God" (Luke 16:15).

A third way of hindering the Spirit is by intentionally pushing Him away. In these cases Satan takes over to make sure that the Spirit is diverted. For Satan is threatened by truly spiritual worship, and he will do anything to hold us back. One of his methods is to plant people in the congregation whose very presence will divert and hinder the Spirit. And these people know what they are doing. At Satan's instigation people will sometimes call out during the service. There may be a drunk or a demon-possessed person in the congregation. In a congregation of many people even one individual can hinder the work of the Spirit. Not to believe that is to misunderstand how the Spirit acts.

One summer I was preaching in a church in the Florida Keys, and as I began to talk about the blood of Jesus, someone who had been brought along specially to hear me preach began to call out to me in a very strange voice. It got worse and worse until finally I told everybody to bow their heads. We sang a chorus while the person was removed, and at once the atmosphere changed. You could feel the presence of God, and by the time we finished the service, some had even forgotten what had happened.

We are engaged in warfare against Satan. Ephesians 6:12 says, "For our fight is not against flesh and blood, but against principalities, against powers, against the rulers of the darkness of this world." All of us need to be aware of Satan's ways of hindering the Spirit during worship, and I will be looking at this in more detail in Chapter 15.

How, then, do we *honor* the Spirit? We must never forget that He is a person, the third person of the Trinity, and we must respect Him. We must learn, first of all, to respect His sensitivity. Many people do not realize that He is easily grieved, easily offended, and easily quenched. I do not mean that He is sensitive in the way proud people are sensitive. There are many people to whom you hardly dare speak because you are always putting your foot in it and injuring their feelings in some way. No, the Holy Spirit is sensitive, if only because He is so utterly pure and holy. He cannot be free to work where there is sin, and there is sin wherever people are depending on themselves instead of coming to Jesus for forgiveness and power to live their lives.

But we must respect not only the Spirit's sensitivity but also

His impartiality. He is "no respecter of persons" (Acts 10:34). He cannot be bought; He cannot be paid off; He cannot be influenced. You can't make any secret deals with Him. Many people seem to think—often without even realizing they think it—that if they have been a Christian, perhaps a deacon or a preacher, for a very long time, then they can come to an understanding with the Spirit and be granted a special indemnity on the basis of past service.

But you can be a Christian for thirty years and find He is no longer working in you because you have suddenly grieved Him, while someone who has been converted less than six months can have the Spirit in great power and be much used by God. You may think that this is not fair on a Christian who has "borne the burden and the heat of the day" (Matt. 20:12). But Jesus said, "So the last will be first, and the first last" (Matt. 20:16). The Spirit is no respecter of persons.

We must also respect and obey the Spirit's impulse. That is, as we saw in Chapter 2, we must let Him be Himself in us. This means that we must let Him be Himself in others too. We ought not to judge the style of another person's worship.

Some of our fathers were given great discernment and could recognize the presence of the Spirit. The man whom God used more than any other in the Welsh Revival was Evan Roberts. But for a year or two before the revival began, many people were worried about Evan Roberts. They thought there was something strange about him.

But then a man arrived who had been present fifty years before, at the Welsh Revival of 1859, and who knew something of the ways of the Spirit. And when he heard that people were criticizing Evan Roberts, he said, "Don't put a hand on that boy. God is dealing with him." He could recognize the work of the Spirit.

One of my childhood memories is of a two-week meeting in my church in Ashland. On the last night they brought in one of the greatest preachers I had ever heard. And the place was packed, with everybody waiting expectantly to hear the sermon.

But when he walked into the pulpit the man just said, "God is here." Then he began singing a simple chorus about how wonderful Jesus is.

Everybody began to sing with him, and God's power was present there. Within about ten minutes fifty or sixty people must have spontaneously stood up and walked down to kneel at the front. Yet that man didn't even preach. Most preachers want to deliver a sermon that they have worked hard to prepare because, after all, people have come to hear them speak. But this man recognized the Spirit and knew that it was far more important to release Him than to preach.

This brings me to the final point: we honor the Spirit by releasing Him. Jesus said, "He who believes in Me, as the Scripture has said, out of his heart shall flow rivers of living water" (John 7:38). Many of us think only in terms of the Spirit coming down, but He can flow out from a well deep within us.

How do we release the Spirit, both in ourselves and in others? In ourselves it will happen when we keep peace in our hearts with everybody we know. Sometimes we play games with ourselves and pretend we are at peace and that all is fine. It is like someone who loses his temper and then says, "I'm not mad." We can justify ourselves until we are a hundred, but the Spirit will never be Himself in us as long as we are unforgiving, judgmental, prejudiced, or speaking evil of anyone. He will not be Himself in us as long as we are preoccupied with what others are going to think of what we do. It may mean apologizing to someone, or it may be a little thing like raising your hand in worship, but obeying His impulse is all part of honoring the Spirit and releasing Him in ourselves.

And we can release the Spirit in others when we relinquish our control over other people. We can refuse to let another person be afraid of us or admire us too much. (We never do anyone a favor by letting them admire us too much, for sooner or later we will disappoint them.) Or we can refuse to let other people feel under an obligation to us. The flesh, you see, always wants to control. Some ministers want to control their congregations, and some leaders of house churches want to be in control. But the Spirit gives liberty, and through Him we must release others to be themselves—to think for themselves. There may be people who are in bondage just because they are afraid of us, but we can help them. And when we do, the Spirit will be released to be Himself in all of us.

If you are wondering what on earth all this has got to do with the worship service, then I would repeat that worship is not primarily a matter of outward form. It is a matter of the heart. So what we have been talking about has everything to do with the worship service. What happens in our personal lives cannot be divorced from the Spirit's work in public worship.

I was named after my father's favorite preacher—R. T. Williams. I grew up hearing about him, and he must have been a remarkable man. When old Dr. Williams spoke to young men whom he had just ordained into the ministry, he always said the same thing: "Young men, honor the blood. And honor the Holy Ghost."

In the days of revival those whom God used were able to recognize the Spirit and honor Him. They would not get in His way—even if it meant not preaching.

Suppose five hundred people, all of whom possessed the ungrieved Spirit—or rather, all of whom were possessed by the ungrieved Spirit—were to come together to worship? I would love to know what would happen. It could be a spontaneous combustion such as no nuclear explosion has ever produced!

CHAPTER 4

FELLOWSHIP

They continued steadfastly in...fellowship.

—Acts 2:42

I T IS SOMETIMES said that British people are characterized by the "stiff upper lip." This means that when someone hurts you, you never show it so that the person who hurts you doesn't even know.

Often when we grieve the Holy Spirit, we only realize weeks or even months later that we have hurt Him. I define *spirituality* as "the ability to close the time gap between the moment we sin and the moment we realize that we have sinned and therefore grieved the Holy Spirit." Some of us are so proud and self-willed and so sure that we are right that it takes us years before we realize what we have done. But we can learn to bring the time gap down to seconds, and even catch ourselves before we sin, and so avoid grieving the Spirit.

In the last chapter I talked about grieving the Spirit, and I want to continue with this, looking particularly at the subject of fellowship and the bitterness of spirit that destroys fellowship.

You may say, "What on earth has that to do with worship?" And I would reply: "Everything. You just cannot worship in the Spirit if you are out of sorts with your fellow Christians."

When Paul said in Ephesians 4:30, "And do not grieve the Holy Spirit of God, in whom you are sealed for the day of redemption," the very next thing he said was, "Let all bitterness, wrath, anger, outbursts, and blasphemies, with all malice, be taken away from you. And be kind one to another, tenderhearted, forgiving one another, just as God in Christ also forgave you" (vv. 31–32).

You may think, "Well, God understands that I have always had a problem with forgiving people." But you don't have any more of a problem than anybody else: "No temptation has taken you except what is common to man" (1 Cor. 10:13). You may justify your hurt, but in doing so you grieve the Holy Spirit.

Now bitterness can be directed towards God, towards others, or towards ourselves. We are bitter towards God if we get angry about what He has allowed to happen. This prevents us worshipping by the Spirit because we can't worship God very well if we are angry with Him.

Bitterness towards others comes when we are hurt over what they have done to us, and we feel bitterness towards ourselves when we cannot forgive ourselves for what we have done. This shows that we have not accepted the promise, "If we confess our sins, He is faithful and just to forgive us our sins and cleanse us from all unrighteousness" (1 John 1:9). We are trying to dictate to God when we refuse to forgive ourselves when He has forgiven us.

I know what it is to be bitter—and to be bitter for a long time. And I know what it is to justify myself all the time by saying, "God understands." He does. But all the time we are being bitter, the Holy Spirit is being grieved, and we will not know His impulse within us.

A verse which people often prefer to ignore in this connection is 1 Peter 3:7: "Likewise, you husbands, live considerately with your wives, giving honor to the woman as the weaker vessel, since they too are also heirs of the grace of life, *so that your prayers will not be hindered*" (emphasis added).

It is so easy for a husband to get very annoyed with his wife. She may be late doing something, perhaps, or she may get something wrong, and he feels upset. He decides to read his Bible and pray for a while, and it doesn't seem to occur to him that his prayers may be hindered. He simply says to himself, "I'm going to pray. Here I go: Heavenly Father, I'm just going to trust You. I'm mad at her! But You understand, and You'll give me a verse here today. Oh, here's one. No, I don't like that verse. I think I'll read this one…" And all the time the Spirit is grieved.

If a husband is sensitive, he will know that he will not be able to get on with praying until he has got things right again with his wife. I remind you of the statement made by a psychologist from UCLA. He said that after twenty five years of marriage counseling, he had come to the conclusion that in most all cases of trouble it is the man's fault.

First Peter 3:7 states a general principle; it applies, of course, to the wife, and it also operates in the office, a university, or a school. It prohibits any bitterness toward your boss, a colleague, or a school friend.

You may be thinking by now, "Well, this is pretty difficult."

It is. That is precisely why the people whom God has used in history are signally rare. But it needn't be that way. If only the congregations in our churches lived like this seven days a week, then, when they came together to sing the hymns and participate in the Lord's Supper, the worship wouldn't be a mockery.

The earliest record of any pattern of worship is found in Acts 2:42, where we have a description of what immediately followed the baptism of the three thousand people who were saved after Peter's sermon on the day of Pentecost. It says, "They continued steadfastly in the apostles' teaching and fellowship, in the breaking of bread and in the prayers."

From this verse you can see the importance of fellowship in the worshipping life of the early church. If fellowship is not present, worship ceases. But what constituted fellowship? The answer is that two things were shared: a common faith and a common enemy. Three thousand people may seem like a good number, but compared to the hundreds of thousands who were in Jerusalem at that time, it was a very small minority.

These three thousand all believed in the resurrection of Jesus. They had all just been baptized and were full of the Holy Spirit.

And they were hated by the religious and secular leaders. But in face of this opposition they had each other.

We know that the world has nothing in common with us, and we come together to be with people who share what we believe. In the early church no one was at odds with anyone else at first. There was such power present that they were actually detached from their worldly possessions (Acts 2:44).

The world looked on and sensed that something special was happening. Acts 5:13 says, "No one else dared join them." The non-Christian Jews were in awe of Christians at the time, and they could not join them unless the Holy Spirit brought them in.

That is what is needed today, but it is impossible when people in church avoid each other. Jonathan Edwards said that Satan had training in the greatest university that ever was—the heaven of heavens.[1] And oh, the devil knows how to hinder the moving of the Spirit! It is not enough to sing hymns or to listen to preaching or to be sound in doctrine. If we want New Testament worship, then we must see that fellowship is a vital and necessary ingredient of worship.

We also see from Acts 2:42 that in the early Christian community there was preaching (the apostles' teaching), breaking of bread, and prayer, and I will look at these in following chapters. But it is interesting to note here the order of these things: doctrine, fellowship, and then the Lord's Supper and prayer. This indicates that we have no right to partake of the Lord's Supper when we are out of fellowship with others who are present. We will not be able to worship God if we have not made an attempt to put things right. As we have seen, we grieve the Holy Spirit if it is within our power to release another person by what we say and yet we do nothing about it.

I know there are times when we just can't sort things out. We can talk to some people for hours and get nowhere with them. But at least we have followed the New Testament pattern and tried. Paul said, "If it is possible, as much as it depends on you, live peaceably with all men" (Rom. 12:18). Our heavenly Father loves all of us equally. However, what is important is that we ourselves should not be harboring animosity and bitterness.

Acts 2 concludes with this lovely description of the early church: "And continuing daily with one mind in the temple, and breaking bread from house to house, they ate their food with gladness and simplicity of heart, praising God and having favor with all the people. And the Lord added to the church daily those who were being saved" (vv. 46–47).

When in our worship there is fellowship and love, then the joy we experience flows out into a life of praise and witness.

CHAPTER 5

WORSHIP, PREACHING, AND THE PREACHER

They continued steadfastly in the apostles' teaching.

—ACTS 2:42

IN MY OPINION, the call to preach is the highest calling in the world and the highest honor that God can bestow on any man. There is a sense in which preaching is the most tangible link between men and the triune God.

But it is also the greatest responsibility that there is. Charles Spurgeon used to give this advice to any who were undecided about whether or not they ought to become ministers of the gospel: "If you can do anything else, do it."[1] He meant that, if you can succeed at anything else, then you are not called to preach. On the other hand, a minister who *is* called would be like a fish out of water anywhere except in the pulpit.

Let me remind you of our definition of *worship*: it is "the response to, and/or preparation for, the preached Word." This definition obviously makes preaching central to worship. This was one of the discoveries made way back in the sixteenth century. The rediscovery of justification by faith was only one part of the great Reformation. There was also a rediscovery of preaching, for in the Middle Ages the emphasis had been on the sacraments.

It is quite wrong to refer to the singing—both hymns and choruses—as though they alone comprise the worship. This is easy to do. We tend to think of the morning and evening service as if it is divided into two parts: first the worship, and then the preaching.

We must, of course, never underestimate the importance and the impact of singing, and I will be devoting two chapters to music and singing. There is music and singing in heaven. God can speak through the hymns, and we worship Him in them. Our English hymnody is unexcelled in the world, and I spend considerable time choosing the hymns in order to get them exactly right. But the thrust and pinnacle of worship lies in the preaching. In the Book of Acts, which is the earliest historical account of the church, the emphasis is not on singing. It is not even on the Lord's Supper. On every page—almost, it seems, on every other line—the emphasis is on preaching.

In this chapter I want us to see not only the centrality of preaching in worship, but that preaching should itself be worship. Even as the preacher speaks, we should all be worshipping. How can this be true? Well, simply because preaching is God's chosen way to save people. Paul says in 1 Corinthians 1:21: "For since, in the wisdom of God, the world through its wisdom did not know God, it pleased God through the foolishness of preaching to save those who believe." It doesn't say, "through foolish preaching," although there is enough of that around. It says, "through the foolishness of preaching." And when Paul wrote to Titus, he said that God "has in due time revealed His word through preaching" (Titus 1:3).

Here is a very simple definition of *preaching*: "God's Word reaching man through human personality." The chief thing about preaching is that it must bring a real sense of God, not just of the Word of God but of God Himself. And we will never worship unless that happens. So Paul could say in 1 Corinthians 2:4–5: "My speech and my preaching was not with enticing words of man's wisdom, but in demonstration of the Spirit and of power, so that your faith should not stand in the wisdom of men, but in the power of God."

God uses ordinary men, and the preacher's personality actually becomes the very instrument of God. But for this to happen, the preacher must be called, prepared, uncontrived, and unafraid. If he does not have these characteristics, there will be bad preaching.

It is possible to have good speaking but bad preaching. Notice that in the verse I have just quoted, Paul refers to "my speech and my preaching." He distinguished between the two. It is possible to be only speaking and not actually preaching, even though it may be called preaching.

And it is also possible for there to be bad speaking but good preaching. In 2 Corinthians 10:10, Paul refers to the way some of the people at Corinth talked about him. We read, "'For his letters,' they say, 'are weighty and powerful, but his bodily presence is weak, and his speech contemptible.'" They thought his speaking amounted to nothing. Imagine anyone saying that about the great apostle Paul!

For worship to take place through preaching, there must be soundness, urgency, and relevance. The preaching must also be gripping and effectual. We can visualize preaching as a pyramid with five layers representing soundness, relevance, urgency, the ability to grip the hearer, and, at the pinnacle, an effectual quality. Preaching which is "by the impulse of the Spirit" must have all these five elements. However, preaching can display the first four of these qualities without the Holy Spirit. But preaching will only be effectual if the Holy Spirit is present.

Sound preaching is preaching that is theologically and biblically correct. Paul said, "For I determined not to know anything among you except Jesus Christ and Him crucified" (1 Cor. 2:2). This was at the heart of all his preaching. And all theology, rightly understood, comes down to that: "Jesus Christ and Him crucified." The importance of sound teaching must never be underestimated, and a preacher's exegesis—his interpretation of Scripture—*must* be correct.

The second level, relevance, means that the preaching ought to touch the lives of the listeners. Look how Paul puts it: "My speech and my preaching was not with enticing words of man's wisdom, but in demonstration of the Spirit and of power, so that your faith should not stand in the wisdom of men, but in the power of God" (1 Cor. 2:4–5). Paul was determined that his preaching should relate to the faith of his hearers.

But that is not enough. There must be urgency. Paul said, "I was with you in weakness and in fear and in much trembling" (1 Cor. 2:3). This was because of the urgency he felt. The preacher must long for the hearers to understand what is meant and why it *must* be believed.

And the preaching must also be gripping—that is, it must stir the heart of the listeners. It must break through defensive barriers.

But preaching that is gripping may still be ineffectual. In Acts 24:24–25 we read, "After several days, when Felix arrived with his wife Drusilla, who was a Jewess, he sent for Paul and heard him speak concerning faith in Christ. As he lectured about righteousness, self-control, and the coming judgment, Felix was afraid and answered, 'For now, leave! When time permits, I will send for you.'"

Where Felix was concerned, Paul's preaching was not effectual. And this can be the case not only when the preaching is to non-Christians but also when it is to Christians in the Sunday services. I am quite sure that many people are often gripped by the Sunday sermon, but they just think, "I'm not ready to do that yet." Like Felix, they say, "When time permits, I will send for you."

When preaching is effectual, worship takes place, for then the preaching is not with the words of man's wisdom but by the demonstration of the Spirit and of power so that the listener is caught up into the heavenlies and loses sight of everything but God's voice. Some people may even start to laugh or to cry while the preacher is speaking, but the intercourse between God and man goes on unbroken. And this is what every preacher longs for.

Effectual preaching leads to repentance, which means "a change of mind leading to a change of life." For one person this may mean a one hundred eighty degree turn, whereas for another, who is already walking in the light, it may lead to only a slight shift in direction.

Sometimes only one person in a congregation responds with repentance, or maybe hundreds will, and this is a time of great rejoicing indeed. Then the preacher and the listener are in the Spirit, and a surge of heaven—a wave of glory—sweeps over the congregation so that everyone knows that everyone else feels the same way. This is what we mean when we speak of unction.

The preacher may be aware of three things while he is preaching. Sometimes he may feel nothing at all—yet the congregation feels the presence of God's Spirit. The preacher may be like Moses, who did not know "the glory of his countenance" (2 Cor. 3:7). I think there are few things more encouraging (it has happened to me more than once) than to leave the pulpit feeling an utter failure, only to find that after all someone was spoken to or converted.

But sometimes when I am preaching I enjoy myself considerably—only to come down from the pulpit and find I was the only one!

Thirdly, and joy of joys, is when the preacher and congregation together are filled with a sense of the presence of where there is the unction I have just referred to. This is a weighty responsibility for the minister because up to a point he can control this surge of the Spirit. It is a great mystery, but it is absolutely true. This is another reason why Paul said, "I was with you in weakness and in fear and in much trembling" (1 Cor. 2:3).

I can tell you these things because I have learned them by sad and happy experience. I know what it is to have the Spirit working in great power in me—I can feel it when I am preaching. And when that happens, I know I must do two things. First, I must follow the impulse of the Spirit, and second, I must not try to control what is happening or intrude myself in any way. For at these times there is a warfare going on in the pulpit, and Satan will do anything he can to divert me. He may, for example, cause me to hear a noise or to notice a particular look on someone's face. Or the temptation may come to say something I ought not to say. If I give in, the surge of the Spirit will suddenly diminish. I have quenched Him myself and have kept my congregation bound instead of releasing them.

Finally, to be honest about what can happen when someone is preaching, I ought to include a fourth possibility: the preacher may feel nothing and the people may feel nothing! But I hope that doesn't happen too often.

Preaching that is by the Spirit of God occurs when the Spirit works through the preacher without any hindrance. For this to happen, there must first be no self-righteousness in the preacher. The moment he puts himself up on a pedestal as if he thinks he is better than his congregation, he will lose all his effectiveness.

Second, he must not preach at anyone directly because this is always counterproductive. One of the temptations a minister faces is to preach in a special way if he knows a certain person is in the congregation. There's not a minister in the world who doesn't know what I am talking about here. But nine times out of ten, when I have given in to this temptation and planned a special sermon, the person I thought would be present has not turned up! I think this is due to the mercy of God, because I know that every time I do a thing like that, I am ineffective. One can be effective only when one is oblivious of who is present. Only then will the listeners be set free.

Third, the preacher must not inject any private opinions into his sermons.

Fourth, he must bring no grudges whatsoever into the pulpit. It is only too possible to preach while harboring grievances—I know; I've done it myself. But at those times I've not had any anointing.

Finally, the preacher must say what he knows the Spirit wants him to say, even if it is not going to be popular.

But all this means that the minister's life must be given over to God twenty-four hours a day, seven days a week. The greatest folly of any preacher is to think that he can become the vehicle of God just by stepping into the pulpit; this can only come about as the outflow of a lifestyle. Every pastor and clergyman should ask himself: "Do I please God? What if the people really did follow me and every member of my church were just like me? What if they prayed no more than I did? What if they forgave those who hurt them only to the extent that I forgave?" It is a sobering thought.

My first five years at Westminster Chapel were pleasant and uneventful. But then a great change came over my ministry. What changed it all was something which happened to me in the manse at midnight on April 14, 1982. Arthur Blessitt had spent the evening with us, and we were on our knees praying. I asked Arthur to pray that I would have unction. I reckoned that, if I could get such a man as Arthur to pray for me, God would really answer the prayer. But Arthur just said to me, "You know, unction is not something that only comes when you walk into a pulpit; it's what flows out of a life."

And Arthur thought he had hurt me and had lost a friend by saying that. But it was what I most needed to hear. I saw that night that something had to happen to me. A fundamental change was required in me. And I died a thousand deaths. I had wanted something to happen when I went into the pulpit, but God showed me it wasn't going to be that way. I had to change. And I have never been the same since.

However, suppose that all I have described in this chapter has happened. Suppose the Word has gone out in the power of the Spirit from a preacher who is living in the power of the Spirit. It is possible that those listening may still not be converted or led into worship. This is because a very great responsibility also lies with the congregation. And this is what I want to turn to in the next chapter.

CHAPTER 6

WORSHIP AND LISTENING

Faith comes by hearing, and hearing by the word of God.

—ROMANS 10:17

W HAT CAN BE more important than correct listening? We only worship God to the degree that we hear Him speak. This is why there are injunctions throughout Scripture about hearing and listening. Jesus would frequently end a parable with the words, "He who has ears to hear, let him hear" (e.g. Luke 8:8). The psalmist said, "Today if you hear His voice, do not harden your hearts, as at Meribah" (Ps. 95:7–8). This was echoed in Hebrews 3:8. There is also the warning in Hebrews 5:11. Here the writer says in effect: "I was getting ready to talk to you about Melchizedek, but I can't go on, seeing that I have many difficult things to say and you are hard of hearing."

Isaiah said, "Seek the LORD while He may be found, call you upon Him while He is near." (Isa. 55:6).

What we are talking about is the ability to recognize and respond to the Spirit's impulse. I consider this to be the highest level of spirituality that exists.

Are we able to see the work of the Spirit? Would we recognize revival if we saw it or heard about it? If God poured out His Spirit in some unexpected place, would we still recognize Him? Do we know when God is speaking to us? Can we sense the way He is leading us? The spiritual ability to recognize the Spirit's impulse comes from listening to and hearing God.

I want to approach this subject from the general and then

move on to the particular. By *general* I mean knowing how to listen to God anywhere—at home, at work, on a train, seven days a week, twenty-four hours a day.

I would like to put to you a premise that is hard to accept, yet is thrilling and true: God is trying to get us to listen to Him. It was Alexander Maclaren who said, "We can have as much of God as we want."[1] Some people may deny this. They say that if it were true, they would know it. But it is affirmed seven times in Revelation chapters 2 and 3. Each time Jesus gave a particular word to the church, He added, "Hear what the Spirit says to the churches." God is constantly trying to get the churches' attention.

It's very interesting that after Jesus addressed all seven churches with the words, "Hear what the Spirit says," He then narrowed the invitation down to one person and said, "If anyone hears My voice and opens the door, I will come in and dine with him, and he with Me" (Rev. 3:20).

Someone may protest, "My problem is getting God to listen to me. I identify with the psalmist when he said, 'Hear me when I call, O God of my righteousness! You have given me relief when I was in distress; have mercy on me, and hear my prayer' (Ps. 4:1). That's where I am. I'm always asking God to hear me."

Maybe you feel like the people who said, "O God, we have fasted and You didn't even notice!" (See Isa. 58:3.) It is possible to spend hours every day talking to God like this. But the problem is that it is *we* who are doing all the talking, all the thinking, and all the groaning, and we shut God out. We think we are open to Him when in fact we are only talking to Him. And all the time He may be wanting to communicate with us at the level that we need, not at the level at which we are addressing Him. We want to talk about one thing and God is saying, "That's not your problem; your problem is over here." We are looking in one direction, and He's trying to get us to look in another.

Now when anyone develops a hearing problem, it usually

doesn't happen overnight. It is a gradual and almost unnoticed event. And the same thing is true at the spiritual level: we hardly know it is happening. In the end we have to be jolted and made to realize what has been going on. It is like not realizing we have been asleep until we wake up.

There are two reasons why God has difficulty in getting us to listen to Him. The first is our inability to absorb or take in His counsel. Jesus said it like this: "I have yet many things to tell you, but you cannot bear them now" (John 16:12). His disciples wouldn't have admitted to that. They would have said, "Try, me. See if I can't take it. Speak plainly." But Jesus said, "You couldn't take it." We all overestimate our capacity to grasp and take in things, not realizing that if God were to tell us all there is to know, our minds would snap. God has to deal with us where we are.

People come into the vestry and say, "Do you think you know what my problem is?"

Many years ago I made the mistake of saying to one person, "Yes, I think I do."

This person said, "Well, what is it?"

It was an awful moment. I said, "I think we ought to talk a little more over several weeks."

He said, "Come on. Tell me. I can take it."

So I told him.

He said, "You are direct, aren't you?" And he never came back.

I should have known better. From many years of pastoral experience I have learned that people don't want their problems solved. They want them understood. We are all like that, and God knows it.

The second reason why God has difficulty in getting us to listen to Him is that there is uncleansed sin within us as a result of not walking in the light. We say, "Lord, speak to me."

God answers, "I did speak, but you wouldn't take it."

We say, "I didn't want that. Lord, speak to me."

"I am speaking."

"No, Lord, speak to me."

A lady once came to Arthur Blessitt and asked him, "Why doesn't God speak to me like He seems to speak to you?"

And Arthur said to her, "Did you ever feel the impulse to speak to a stranger about the Lord but then were ashamed and didn't do it?"

When the lady replied, "Yes, I have," Arthur said, "Well, that's your problem. When you start to obey the impulse of the Spirit, God's voice gets clearer and clearer."

God is trying to reach us, and we hear Him to the degree that we are walking in the light. Is it possible that God is trying to speak to you along a certain line but you are saying, "I know God wouldn't say that to me"?

Here's a verse that none of us likes: "Then they also will answer Him, 'Lord, when did we see You hungry or thirsty or a stranger or naked or sick or in prison, and did not serve You?' He will answer, 'Truly I say to you, as you did it not for one of the least of these, you did it not for Me.'" (Matt. 25:44–45). When we get to the judgment, the Lord could look at us in much the same way and remind us of certain areas of our life, and we will be speechless. It's very important that we should be transparently honest with ourselves.

The final tragic result of disobedience, of course, is that God stops speaking to us. One of the saddest verses in the Bible is 1 Samuel 28:15, where Saul says, "God has departed from me and does not answer me any longer."

There are two kinds of listening: active listening and passive listening.

By *passive listening* I mean when we suddenly, unexpectedly hear the voice of God without planning it or seeking it. If there is a combination of a good knowledge of God's Word plus obedience, then the ecstatic breakthrough may come and come quite unexpectedly. Hearing God in this way happens less frequently than hearing God as a result of active listening, but most of us want only passive listening. We want God to seek us out. That way we don't work hard at hearing God, but when

He taps us on the shoulder, we say, "Praise the Lord! He's still speaking to me."

But passive hearing is not the primary way God speaks to us. God calls us to active listening: "Hear what the Spirit says...." The writer to the Hebrews said, "But solid food belongs to those who are mature, for those who through practice have powers of discernment that are trained to distinguish good from evil" (Heb. 5:14). Exercised senses come through active listening.

The first quality required for active listening is an open mind. That means a mind closed to nothing that coheres with holiness. Paul says about this, "Finally, brothers, whatever things are true, whatever things are honest, whatever things are just, whatever things are pure, whatever things are lovely, whatever things are of good report, if there is any virtue, and if there is any praise, think on these things" (Phil. 4:8).

The second prerequisite for active listening is a willingness to let go of our pride, a willingness to be vulnerable. Jesus said to the church of the Laodiceans, "For you say, 'I am rich, and have stored up goods, and have need of nothing,'" and the truth is, says Jesus, "you are wretched, miserable, poor, blind, and naked" (Rev. 3:17). I sometimes think that revival will break out when Christians are willing to lose face. Jesus said, "He who loses his life for My sake will find it" (Matt. 10:39).

The third characteristic is that we are always listening out for God's voice, even when this involves a telling off. Jesus said, "Those whom I love, I rebuke and discipline. Therefore be zealous and repent" (Rev. 3:19). God may speak to us through a friend or a stranger, through unanswered prayer, or through the withholding of vindication. It may be through illness. It may be through a hymn: "Sometimes a light surprises the Christian while he sings..."[2] It may be through disappointment. It can be simply because you see the need. If we are really walking in the light, we will look anywhere for God's way of speaking.

Unfortunately, many of us say, "If I have to believe that anybody could be God's instrument in my life, then forget it. There are some people I draw the line at." Yet Paul said, "I am a debtor...both to the wise and to the unwise" (Rom. 1:14).

Sometimes we deceive ourselves without realizing it. We think we are openly and actively listening to God, when we are actually blinkered. As I have said, so often we expect God to speak to us in one way, when all the time He is approaching us differently. Someone has put it like this: God gives hints rather than directions. He lets you come to the conclusion for yourself.

John the Baptist wanted more than a hint; he wanted clear direction. In prison he had a moment of discouragement, even though once he had said, "Look, the Lamb of God, who takes away the sin of the world" (John 1:29). He had second thoughts and sent back word to Jesus, "Are You the One who is coming, or shall we look for another?" (Luke 7:19). Imagine John the Baptist talking like that! You would have thought that Jesus would have replied: "Tell John, yes, I'm the One." But He didn't answer like that. He just said, "Go and tell John what you have seen and heard: that the blind see, the lame walk, the lepers are cleansed, the deaf hear, the dead are raised, and the gospel is preached to the poor" (Luke 7:22). This was a clear hint. And that's the way God deals with all of us.

The fourth prerequisite to hearing God is that we deal with any impediment that militates against the Spirit—for example, any personal bias which we superimpose upon God, calling it His will when it's actually our own prejudice, and any grudge or unforgiving attitude.

I remember receiving a letter from a lady I had never met but who had heard me preach on Joseph and his brothers. I preached on the concept of total forgiveness, by which I mean totally forgiving the other person, no matter who it is or what has been done. I said that, to the degree you don't forgive, no matter how wronged you are, you are the one in chains.

She wrote me a long letter saying, "Let me tell you what's happened to me...." A relative had done something really wicked twenty-five years ago, and this lady said, "I can't forgive, but your sermon made me wonder if I should."

I wrote back and said, "You must."

Some weeks later she wrote again and said, "I never thought I could do it, but I did and the joy is wonderful."

We may justify our hurt and say that God is angry too. We may think He is because that's the way we want Him to feel, but He's not going to bend the rules for us, even if we are in the right. Total forgiveness is our only way out. If we walk in the light, we are going to have to forgive. If we don't forgive, there will be uncleansed sin.

Another impediment that militates against hearing God speaking is when we superimpose our traditions upon the Word of God. This is what the Pharisees did when they made the word of God of no effect through their traditions (Matt. 16:6). I will be returning to this subject in Chapter 21.

Again, we must beware of any fleshly appetite that dulls our spiritual outlook: it may be a television program, our choice of reading, or our choice of friends. Some things may not be bad in themselves, but we know that they dull our desire for God. Though others may think we are silly, we know that if we want to hear God's voice consistently and clearly, we must be willing to give some things up.

Finally, as we have already seen, we must obey that impulse of the Spirit which we know leads to holiness and brings honor and glory to God. If we don't obey, we become hard of hearing and gradually don't hear God saying, "This is the way, walk in it" (Isa. 30:21).

To sum up the difference between active and passive listening: active listening is reading the Bible without feeling any inspiration. There are times when we don't feel like reading the Bible. We think, "Oh, Lord, I don't want to read Your Word today." But we go on and read God's Word in spite of our feelings, because Paul said, "Be ready in season and out of season" (2 Tim. 4:2).

When we learn to develop a lifestyle of active listening, we will hear God's voice much more frequently than before because now we are beginning to recognize when He speaks.

I know from personal experience that it can sometimes take an embarrassing number of years before we recognize that God has been speaking to us. Eventually we say, "That really was God speaking to me then. I didn't know it, but I see now it was."

Whenever we have a violent reaction to something, we must be alert to the possibility that God might be wanting to teach us something. We say, "God wouldn't say that to me!" And it might take us ten years before we realize our mistake.

My first reaction to Evangelism Explosion in 1964 was that it was fleshly, and I spoke against Dr. James Kennedy. I'm so ashamed now—but he loved me right through it all.

Let me give you some practical advice: write down in detail a list of questions you would like God to answer. They may be theological or practical. I've done this. I have a prayer list with the theological questions I'm asking. "Lord, tell me the truth about what I should believe in detail about grace or the law. Do I really have to affirm predestination or the doctrine of election? Show me the truth about baptism or what I need to know about hell and heaven or the doctrine of the church." Write them out and pray over them every single day for a year.

Then write out the practical questions. "Lord, do you want me to get this job? Do you want me to go there? Do you want me to apply for this? Do you want me to see this person?" Write them out and pray over them every day for one year. Then twelve months from now, if you spend the time actively listening to God, see how many of your questions have been answered.

To return now to worship and listening to God at church: if we have been listening this way all day, seven days a week, when we come to church, we continue in the same way.

As far as is possible, we must come to church in an open state of mind. Sometimes we come with a very burdened and preoccupied heart, and we forget how difficult it is for God to speak to us when we are like that. It's best if we can put our own concerns in suspension so that God can speak to us in the way He wants to. It may then turn out that He will deal with the problem we had.

We must come expecting God to speak to us. We must trust the Holy Spirit to have directed the preacher in his choice of hymns or choruses, the reading, the preaching, and the sermon material. And we must receive God's Word with openness and humility. We must, of course, listen critically to what the preacher is saying. No minister should produce a congregation of rubber stamps—that would cut right across the doctrine of the priesthood of all believers. Each person in the congregation must think for himself or herself and assess whether what the preacher is saying is true or not. But if we listen with a defensive, aggressive, or spiteful attitude, then we will quench the Spirit before He can even speak.

Then, we must listen prayerfully—we must know the art of listening and praying at the same time. We must always be aware that powers from below would work against the preaching. So we must pray continually for the preacher as he preaches, and for ourselves to have the grace to receive what the Spirit is saying. The minister and his congregation are all in it together. It is not just a matter of saying, "I wonder if he's going to preach well today." Someone who is only a sermon taster will not worship God.

But if we come longing to hear God speaking to us, actively and prayerfully listening for Him in humility and dependence on His Spirit, then true worship will take place.

CHAPTER 7

EXPECTANCY

When they had prayed, the place where they
were assembled together was shaken.

—Acts 4:31

I CONCLUDED CHAPTER 6 by talking about how important it is to come to church longing to hear God speaking. This is so crucial that I want to return to it. A vital ingredient of worship is expectancy: believing that something good is going to happen. Nothing is sadder than going to church when you aren't expecting anything to happen or even know that nothing is going to happen. When you feel that way—what a surprise— nothing does happen! Yet so many people throughout the world go to church feeling like that. It is not surprising that churches are closing down. You would be shocked if you knew how many evangelical churches in Britain have not had a conversion in five years—and are not even expecting to see any conversions.

Of course, we have just as great a need for expectancy in our private devotional lives. When you come to read your Bible and pray, do you expect something to happen? The peak moment of my day is when I can be alone with God. I get out my Bible and expect God to speak to me. Every time I open my Bible, I think, "Lord, what are You going to say to me today?"

And when I feel this way and look for God to speak, then He often does. This is how it should be with everyone. No one should come to pray thinking, "Oh, I suppose I've got to pray." How dare we claim to love God if coming to Him is a duty!

In Acts 4 we read that a number of people—we don't know

exactly how many—were gathered together to pray. What is remarkable is what happened as soon as they had finished praying. Verse 31 says, "When they had prayed, the place where they were assembled together was shaken." What an extraordinary comment. Nothing like that had ever happened before. It was not that the people were shaken—though I have no doubt they were—but "the place where they were assembled together was shaken. And they were all filled with the Holy Spirit and spoke the word of God with boldness."

In this passage we have a description of an expectant people—and this for four reasons.

First, they were converted people. Why mention this? It's because I wish to say that, if we ever lose that sense of expectancy, we must recall that we are converted—which means that at least once God did something in our lives. These people, who were filled with the Holy Spirit, had already had that experience once. Never think that something can only happen once. Even the baptism of the Holy Spirit can happen again and again. When you are discouraged and find yourself saying, "I haven't been seeing anything happen to me," remember that you are converted. That ought to keep up your sense of expectancy, for if God saved you and me, He can save anybody.

The second reason why these people were expectant is that they had seen God work recently. In Acts 3 we have the account of the miracle of the healing of the lame man. In a sense this miracle was the worst thing that could have happened to the church. You would think that a miracle would make everybody happy. But not at all. When something like that happens, then all the so-called religious people vent their hatred on the people of God. And I suspect that, if similar miracles were to happen today, they would get the church into just as much trouble.

Everybody had seen God work, not only at the level of healing, but also in the miracle of conversion, which, of course, is the greatest miracle of all. And numbers in the church were growing—Acts 4:4 speaks of "about five thousand" people. It is important for us to see God at work continuously, and it is a wonderful experience when people are converted in our church services. When we have seen God working, we expect Him to continue working.

One of my great joys is fishing. All year I fish for men, but for my summer holiday we go to the Florida Keys and I fish for fish. It is very discouraging to hear people saying, "There's no use going out—no one's catching anything. We were out all day yesterday and got nothing." (Discouraging, that is, unless you're as determined as I am. Nothing will stop me, and I go out anyway!)

But if everyone says, "They're all over the place! Everywhere we were yesterday, there were bonefish tailing on this flat—on that flat...!" Then you go out expecting something to happen. When I hear that, and I know that the wind is right, the tide is right, and the water temperature is right, I get so excited that I can hardly sleep the night before!

It is the same in our churches. When we have seen something happen, as these people in Acts had, we look to God for it to happen again.

But, third, the people had also just seen the devil stirred up. We read in verse 18 that the religious officials had called Peter and John in and "commanded them not to speak or teach at all in the name of Jesus." And the devil was behind that. For whenever the church regroups to evangelize, you can mark it down that the devil will be angry. Many things the church gets involved with pose no threat to the devil, and he stays at bay. But once you propose to invade his territory, you have a fight on your hands. When the devil is stirred up, it is a good sign because it shows he is afraid that something is going to happen.

The final reason why these people were expectant is that they knew what God was able to do. This is why they prayed as they did. Verses 23 and 24 say, "On being released, [Peter and John] went to their own people and reported what the chief priests and elders had said to them. When they heard this, they lifted their voices in unity to God." They had their backs against the wall, but they had a momentum derived from seeing God work beyond the natural level.

Many churches can never think other than at the natural level. What about our resources? Who do we know? Who can pull this string for us? But here was a group who only had God to back them up. Five thousand may sound like a large number of people—but they were a tiny minority in the country at the time—and they were hated and despised by the authorities. They didn't have powerful friends in the Sanhedrin who would stand up for them. They had no one in Caesar's government. But they had God. So they were expectant.

I suspect that most of us haven't a clue about what it really means to be expectant and to rely on God alone. So let's look more closely at this prayer in Acts 4—a prayer that resulted in a building being shaken!

First, in this prayer we see the unity of the people. Verse 24 says that "they lifted their voices in unity to God." Unity is of vital importance in worship. The people here had achieved their unity by coming together against a common enemy. But this unity also required magnanimity. You can be sure that they had differences among themselves—everybody does. (And the less you have of the Spirit, the more important will those differences seem.) But they knew that the devil was against them, so they put their differences aside. Would to God that the church at the present time would do the same.

The issue at stake here was that the witnessing should not stop. The authorities had told Peter and John that they would not be put in prison for what they believed, but that they were to keep it to themselves: "They…commanded them not to speak or teach at all in the name of Jesus" (v. 18). If these early Christians had been like some of us today, someone would have stood up and said, "Look here, Peter and John, we think you're carrying this a bit too far. We've done our piece. We've done a bit of witnessing and shown that we could do it. But now we've upset the Sanhedrin, and they are learned and respected men. So let's cool it for a while."

But not one person said anything like that. Instead, they lifted up their voices to God in unity. If the Church had become divided at that point, the Book of Acts would have ended right there. There is no substitute for witnessing.

The second aspect of the expectancy of these people is that they uttered their longings. They put their words on the line. It is easy to keep one's thoughts to oneself. Other people can't hold us accountable for what we've not said. But these early Christians shared what was in their minds.

The NIV says, "They raised their voices" (v. 24). I don't think I've ever heard that in our church prayer meetings. I never hear more than one person pray at one time. Are we afraid to speak out all at once?

In South Korea the Christians are seeing God at work, and a film has been made about the revival there. In this film we see the minister of a church lead in prayer, and everyone starts praying. I don't suppose the people even knew what the minister was saying. It's a noisy meeting.

Could it be that revival has come to the third world and passed us by because we are too sophisticated? In those churches in South Korea they are not ashamed to cry aloud to God. Most of our praying is shameful: "Heavenly Father, we come to You…we pray for Your blessing upon us and…to have Your way…in our hearts and lives…and… and…"

There is no indication in our language that we expect to see God do anything. I'm not saying that this would bring revival. I'm only saying that this is what they knew in Acts, when the Spirit was present. Perhaps our problem is that we're just too comfortable.

The third thing we can see about this prayer is its upward direction: "They lifted their voices in unity to God" (v. 24). It didn't cross their minds to look to one another. Yes—they talked to one another, but how long do you think the "committee meeting" lasted? Verse 23 says, "On being released, they went to their own people and reported what the chief priests and elders had said to them." I suppose that took about five minutes, and then they were on their faces.

We are in the day of committees and conferences—"the merry-go-rounds of conferences," as it has been put. We don't see God work, but we're great at talking to one another. When these people heard what Peter and John had to say, they didn't have to debate it. They just said, "Let's pray."

I never will forget the night many years ago when Dr. O. S. Hawkins said he would take my wife and me out for a meal after the deacons' meeting at his church. He said, "We'll just be a little while."

I thought he'd be at least a couple of hours, but about twenty-five minutes later he appeared and said, "Are you ready to go?"

When I expressed my surprise that he was so early, he asked me to take a look in at the meeting—and there were twenty-five deacons on their knees, praying. He said, "That's the way our deacons' meetings go."

I fear that the importance of prayer hasn't begun to grip many of our churches like this.

The fourth thing about this prayer is the understanding that undergirded their expectancy. There are three things here. First, what these people understood about God. Verse 24 says, "When they heard this, they lifted their voices in unity to God and prayed, 'Lord, You are God, who has made the heaven and the earth and the sea and everything in them.'" The people knew that God made the world and everything in it: He is the all-powerful Creator.

Secondly, these people believed that God wrote the Bible. Verse 25 says, "Who by the mouth of Your servant David said: 'Why did the nations rage...?'" As Calvin said, one of the best ways to pray is just to quote God's Word back to Him.

The third thing is their belief in God's sovereignty. Verses 27 and 28 say, "Indeed, both Herod and Pontius Pilate, with the Gentiles and the people of Israel, were assembled together against Your holy Son Jesus whom You have anointed, to do what Your hand and Your counsel had foreordained to be done."

This is a crucial point. They saw God in everything. When the Crucifixion took place, the disciples hadn't been able to see God's hand in it at all. All they could say was, "Isn't it horrible that this has happened to Jesus!" But now they could look back and say, "God did it." Satan filled the heart of Judas Iscariot. Wicked men led Pontius Pilate to do what he did. But God was behind it all.

First Corinthians 2:7–8 says, "But we speak the wisdom of God in a mystery, the hidden wisdom, which God ordained before the ages for our glory. None of the rulers of this age knew it. For had they known it, they would not have crucified the Lord of glory."

But Satan always overreaches himself. And the angrier Satan is, the more you ought to look for God's sovereign overruling. These people had seen what God had done through the crucifixion of Jesus, and they could see now that Satan was at work again. But they were not panicking because they knew that Satan never catches God off guard. The expectancy of these early Christians was clothed with a robust view of God's sovereign purposes.

Finally, their expectancy had an urgency. The key word is *now*. Look at Acts 4:29: "Now, Lord, look on their threats." Sometimes God brings us to the place where we have to see Him act *now*. Urgency always means, "Lord, do it now!" They weren't asking for the conditions to be removed so that they wouldn't have to be witnesses any more. They simply wanted boldness to witness, and they prayed for God to do again what He had done before. They had already seen signs and wonders, and that had got them into a heap of trouble, but they said, "Lord, do it again!" They wanted God to give a fresh display of His power.

And God's response to the prayer of the people was that the place was shaken. Never before had they seen anything like it. And it has not occurred since. Sometimes God just likes to do something once. Joshua saw the sun stand still for twenty-four hours. It never happened again. On the day of Pentecost "tongues as of fire" came on the heads of the people (Acts 2:3). It happened once. God may do something with us which will never be repeated. And if our expectancy is at the level of these people in Acts 4, who knows what it might be?

All this was the consequence of their expectancy and trust in God. May God grant that such expectancy may be in all our church services and prayer meetings. Then perhaps we too will see the unprecedented, or at the very least, what we long for: a demonstration of God's power that defies natural explanation.

CHAPTER 8

WORSHIPPING IN THE DARK

Though the fig tree does not blossom, nor fruit be on the vines... yet I will rejoice in the Lord; I will exult in the God of my salvation.

—HABAKKUK 3:17–18

As we have just seen in Chapter 7, expectancy is a vital ingredient in worship. Those who come to church expecting something to happen are more likely to see God work than those who come expecting nothing. But what about when we do come with expectancy and nothing happens? What about when we feel God has let us down? We say, "God, I came today, and I wanted You to speak, but You didn't speak to me!" What can we say about times like these?

The same questions apply to our own quiet times with God. Maybe we've prayed every day during the week and yet have not experienced God's blessing or seen Him answer prayer. What then?

My answer is that faithfulness is, if anything, even more important than expectancy in worship: "It is required in stewards [that is, those who have been given a trust] that a man [or woman] be found faithful" (1 Cor. 4:2). "Who can find a faithful man?" asks the writer of Proverbs (20:6). Anybody can be faithful when prayer is being answered, when the wind is at one's back and everything is going well. But what is one to do when God suddenly hides His face?

We have all experienced this. If you are a new Christian

and haven't yet—you will! "Truly You are a God who hides Yourself, O God of Israel, the Savior," said Isaiah (45:15).

The thing about the hiding of the face of God is that it never comes with advance warning. If only I could say to my church members, "I need to make an announcement. This week it is going to be on Wednesday. At about a quarter past eleven you will notice the withdrawal of the light of God's countenance, and you will feel desperate. You are going to be on the brink of despair. You are going to call upon the name of God and receive no reply. Things are going to go wrong. You will feel utterly deserted. It will happen, as I said, on Wednesday morning."

If I could do that, everyone would brace themselves for it. It would be like getting a hurricane or a storm warning. But the thing about the hiding of God's face is that we don't expect it.

And it can happen when we are not aware that we have done anything wrong. God does, of course, hide His face when we are disobeying Him—but when that happens, we understand it. What is particularly painful is when we are doing our best to walk in the light and God hides His face.

The night before Martin Luther was due to stand before the authorities of Rome, who had charged him with heresy, when everybody had turned their backs on him, he walked the floor of his room and cried out, "O my God, art thou dead?" You would have thought that God would have been especially real to Martin Luther at that time. You would have thought that, since God had chosen Luther to be the man who would turn the world upside down, on that particular night He would have given Luther an extra measure of His Spirit. But Luther felt utterly deserted.

The following day he said the famous words, "Here I stand." It sounds triumphant, but Luther was scared to death.

They asked him, "Dr. Luther, are these your tracts?"

He said, "Yes, they are."

"Will you recant what you have said?"

"Yes, I will if you can show that they are contrary to the

Word of God, but if you can't, here I stand. I can do no other. God help me. Amen."

He was scared to death. He had no sense of God's presence but he was faithful.

I never will forget what I went through way back in 1956. I came back from Trevecca Nazarene College in Nashville to my home in Ashland, Kentucky, with a discovery of the sovereign grace of God. I thought my family would clap their hands and say, "This is marvelous." But no. My family deserted me.

Many years ago, as minister of Westminster Chapel, I thought that if we went on with God and were more involved in evangelism, those who had supported me in the past would be behind me, but many weren't.

We don't understand why it is, but sometimes when we obey God, He seems to desert us. Martin Luther said that you must know God as an enemy before you can know Him as a friend. Until you have experienced the hiding of His face and come out on the other side, you won't really come to know God as a friend.

This was Habakkuk's experience. Habakkuk 2:4 is a famous verse which is quoted three times in the New Testament: "The just shall live by his faith." In the Hebrew this reads: "The just shall live by his faithfulness."

There is an intentional ambiguity here. The faithfulness can be God's faithfulness to us or our faithfulness to God; the verse can be read either way, and it means both. In the Dead Sea Scrolls, discovered in 1947, there is a commentary on Habakkuk 2:4, and it reads, "The just shall live by God's faithfulness." This refers to living by the fact that God is faithful to His promises. It is the way Hebrews 10:38 interprets this verse.

But it can equally describe the faithfulness of the individual himself, who doesn't give up hope. The person who trusts God and lives by His promise to bless is declared righteous in the sight of God. That became one of the main verses Paul used for the doctrine of justification by faith. It applies to the future—to the fact that God will accept us in heaven—but it also applies to the present. God is saying that we are declared righteous now. There is an existential element here. The word *existential* means "existence"—the here and now. What needs to be seen from this verse in Habakkuk is that, as we live by God's faithfulness, we are in each moment being declared righteous.

If we could only see this today, it would set us afire. If, in the moment when we don't see answered prayer, we could just look up to heaven and say, "God, I love You anyway," God would declare us righteous just because our faith pleases Him. That kind of faith has a cleansing result. We feel clean. We don't understand why God lets things happen, but we trust Him anyway.

I want to illustrate this in the context of the Book of Habakkuk. Just before writing these words, "The just shall live by his faithfulness" (2:4), Habakkuk says, "For the vision is yet for an appointed time.... If it delays, wait for it" (v. 3). The key phrase is *if it delays, wait for it.* This principle even applies partly to the second coming of Jesus. Jesus said, "But if that evil servant says in his heart, 'My master delays his coming,' and begins to strike his fellow servants and eat and drink with the drunkards, the master of that servant will come on a day when he does not look for him and in an hour he is not aware of and will cut him in pieces and appoint him his portion with the hypocrites, where there shall be weeping and gnashing of teeth" (Matt. 24:48–51).

When Jesus comes again, or when God comes to fulfill any promise He has made to us, will He find us patiently waiting for Him?

After Jesus was raised from the dead, He addressed five hundred at once (1 Cor. 15:6). And on the Day of Pentecost there were one hundred twenty praying in the Upper Room. I believe more than one hundred twenty people could have been there. I believe that, on the first day when Jesus went to heaven, they all went to Jerusalem to wait for the promised Spirit. There were probably five hundred people, all very excited. Then after a couple of days they began to drift away so that when the Day of Pentecost arrived, there were only one hundred twenty. How do you suppose the others felt when they found out what had happened and realized that they had missed out?

Many people make a commitment in a moment of inspiration and get a good feeling, but months later that dwindles away. There is an appalling lack of commitment in so many. People start out saying, "Yes, Lord," then six months later, where are they? It's true with church attendance, with witness on the streets, with tithing, with prayer.

The wider context of Habakkuk shows that there were those who were complaining that God wasn't acting quickly enough. Habakkuk didn't understand either. Elijah was "a man subject to natural passions as we are" (James 5:17). So was Habakkuk. He had questions and doubts. But though he began with complaint, he ended with rejoicing. Habakkuk 1:2 says, "O Lord, how long shall I cry, and You will not hear?" But at the end of the book Habakkuk says, "The Lord God is my strength; He will make my feet like hinds' feet, and He will make me walk on my high places" (3:19). He began by complaining, and he ended by rejoicing.

What happened between the beginning of the Book of Habakkuk and the end? Someone might say, "Obviously things must have changed." But did they? Look at chapter 3, verses 17–18: "Though the fig tree does not blossom, nor fruit be on the vines; though the yield of the olive fails, and the fields produce no food; though the flocks are cut off from the fold, and there be no herd in the stalls—yet I will rejoice in the Lord; I will exult in the God of my salvation." The basis for the complaint was still there. The very things Habakkuk had complained about, he could still complain about. The fig tree wasn't blossoming. There was no fruit, no herd in the stalls—and yet he was rejoicing. He wasn't complaining now. What changed his mind?

We need to see, first of all, the nature of Habakkuk's complaint. First, he complained about God's slowness: "O Lord, how long shall I cry?" (1:2). It makes me think of that verse in Revelation 6:10 that says, "They cried out with a loud voice, 'How long, O Sovereign Lord, holy and true, until You judge and avenge our blood on those who dwell on the earth?'" In Psalm 13:1 we read, "How long, O Lord? Will You forget me for good? How long will you hide Your face from me?"

The question, "How long?" is a familiar question among us all. For most of us God never acts quickly enough. Have you ever asked the question: Why is God slow? One reason is that He sees the end from the beginning. Knowing how it's going to end up, He is in no hurry. Another reason is that time is on His side. Also, as the Bible says, "With the Lord one day is as a thousand years, and a thousand years as one day" (2 Pet. 3:8). God is in no hurry. He is patient.

And very often we are glad that God is patient. Aren't there times when we thank Him for being slow to anger and rich in mercy? How would we like it if God stepped in the moment we sinned? The time comes later when we blush and say, "God, I'm sorry. I was wrong."

And God says, "I knew you were wrong, but I knew you would eventually see it."

Then we say, "Thank you, Lord, for being so patient with me."

Habakkuk also complained that God did nothing while injustice thrived. The NIV translates 1:3 as: "Why do you make me look at injustice? Why do you tolerate wrongdoing?" Don't think that it's only the atheist who questions God about suffering.

The atheist says, "I'll tell you why I don't believe in God...." And he is proud of himself for corning up with such a devastating question: Why does God allow suffering? But Habakkuk, a godly man, said, "Lord, why do you tolerate wrongdoing?" and for a long time God didn't answer. He was silent.

But then, at last, God stepped in. He told Habakkuk that He would send an evil nation, the Chaldeans, to destroy His people. There does come a time when God acts. One after another the prophets all hoped to see the coming of the Messiah, and eventually, after hundreds of years, the Messiah came. As Paul put it: "But when the fullness of time came, God sent forth His Son, born from a woman, born under the law" (Gal. 4:4).

In chapter 2 Habakkuk is getting hold of himself. He says, "I'm going to wait and see what God will say." Three things consoled him. The first was that he could see that God saw what he saw: "And the LORD answered me: Write the vision, and make it plain on tablets, that he who reads it may run" (v. 2). What a relief just to know that God sees!

Hagar, when she was ill-treated by Sarah, looked to heaven and said, "You are the God who sees" (Gen. 16:13)—it is one of the most moving scenes in the Bible.

And that is what God said to Moses: "I have surely seen the affliction of My people" (Exod. 3:7). Nothing is more consoling than to know that God sees. I think that most people come into the vestry to talk to me because they want me to listen and say, "I understand." When we know that God sees, we can make it.

The second thing that consoled Habakkuk was the knowledge that though full intervention might not come as soon as he wanted—"If it delays, wait for it" (Hab. 2:3)—it would nevertheless definitely come. There was a plan; there was a time schedule. God said to Habakkuk: There is an appointed time. Maybe it's a little longer than you want it to be, but wait for it; it will come. That knowledge gave Habakkuk a good feeling.

The third thing that consoled Habakkuk was the understanding that God imputes righteousness to the man or woman who lives by God's faithfulness. We have already observed that this was the foundation for the Pauline doctrine of justification by faith alone. When we say, "God, I don't understand it. I don't know why You have let me wait this long. I don't know why You haven't stepped in sooner. But I am trusting You," we are cleansed in that moment and are given rest of soul. We sense that behind the clouds the sun is shining and God does see us; He says, "I like it when you trust Me that way."

Sometimes in prayer and Bible reading we feel no inspiration, and to continue is almost like drudgery. When I first went to Oxford in 1973, my supervisor, Dr. Barrie White, said, "It's the drudgery of it that you are going to have to endure." And did I have an inferiority complex during those first weeks and months at Oxford! I come from the hills of Kentucky, and I don't think too many people make it to England or Oxford from there. I could see why after I was there. I wondered, "What am I doing here?" I thought, "O God, will I ever get through?" I was at sea, and it was drudgery. I would go every day to the Bodleian Library. I spent twenty-five hours a day in the Bodleian for about two hundred years, it seemed, reading William Perkins and William Ames every day. "Is it worth it?" I asked.

But the breakthrough came. Without the drudgery there would have been no light at the end of the tunnel, no rainbow to trace through the rain. It's when you are faithful daily in everything because it is right that God makes a note of it, and payday comes someday.

At the end of the Book of Habakkuk the prophet is a changed man. Look at his confidence: "Though the fig tree does not blossom, nor fruit be on the vines; though the yield of the olive fails, and the fields produce no food; though the flocks are cut off from the fold, and there be no herd in the stalls—yet I will rejoice in the LORD; I will exult in the God of my salvation. The LORD God is my strength; He will make my feet like hinds' feet, and He will make me walk on my high places" (3:17–19). That is how confident Habakkuk became.

Are you looking for the vine to blossom before you can rejoice? Are you looking for the fig tree to give figs before you can praise the Lord? Are you waiting for the raise in pay? Or for that answered prayer? Are you waiting for everything to fit in before you start praising the Lord? If that is so, then turn in your badge now and give up. As Proverbs 24:10 says, "If you faint in the day of adversity, your strength is small." Here was Habakkuk who still had all these complaints but yet said, "I will rejoice."

Nothing changed outwardly. The basis for Habakkuk's

complaints was still there, the injustices were still there. Nothing had happened to them, but a lot happened to him. Habakkuk was given grace to trace the rainbow through the rain.

Habakkuk saw something that we all need to see: that grace will always be there to keep us one step ahead of the enemy. At the beginning when he talked about the Babylonians, he said, "Their horses are swifter than the leopards" (1:8), but now he says, "[God] will make my feet like hinds' feet" (3:19). Whereas a horse can fun fast, a deer can climb to places a horse cannot reach. Grace will always be given to us so that we can be one step ahead of the enemy. As Moses said, "According to your days, so shall be your strength" (Deut. 33:25).

> The soul that on Jesus has leaned for repose,
> I will not, I will not desert to its foes;
> That soul, though all hell should endeavor to shake,
> I'll never, no never, no never forsake.[1]

Things may not get better around us—but a lot can happen to us—and that changes everything.

CHAPTER 9

WORSHIP AT THE LORD'S TABLE

*They continued steadfastly in the apostles' teaching
and fellowship, in the breaking of bread...*

—ACTS 2:42

No OTHER ACT of worship in the church carries a warning like the one which Paul gives in 1 Corinthians 11:29 concerning the Lord's Supper. Paul says, "For he who eats and drinks unworthily, eats and drinks damnation [Greek: judgment] to himself, not discerning the Lord's body." No such warning is attached to praying or singing, to fellowship or doctrine, important though these are. This shows that the Lord's Supper has an exalted place in God's plan for man.

Yet what do we really know about worship at the Lord's Table? If we don't know a lot, perhaps it will be of some comfort to us to hear that the Christians at Corinth do not seem to have known much. And we can learn from their errors.

In 1 Corinthians 11:17 Paul says, "Now in what I have to say to you, I do not praise you. You have come together not for the better, but for the worse." Or, as the NIV puts it, "I have no praise for you, for your meetings do more harm than good."

In verses 17–32 of chapter 11, Paul mentions three things that were wrong with the church at Corinth, and the first is that there were divisions among them. He says, "For there must also be factions among you so that those who are genuine may become evident among you" (v. 19). I know of no translation of this verse that adequately brings out the fact that Paul is rebuking the Corinthians for maintaining that they needed these divisions and cliques. With biting sarcasm, Paul is saying, "*You* need to have *divisions* to show which of you has God's approval!"

Similarly, back in chapter 4, verse 8, Paul said, "Now you are full, now you are rich; you have begun reigning as kings without us." Here again, Paul is telling the Corinthians off, as we can see from the solemn warning he gives in chapter 4, verses 4–5: "For I know nothing against myself. Yet I am not justified by this. But He who judges me is the Lord. Therefore judge nothing before the appointed time until the Lord comes. He will bring to light the hidden things of darkness and will reveal the purposes of the hearts. Then everyone will have commendation from God." Chapter 11 reveals that the people could not wait for God to show who had His approval. They all thought they knew; each group was convinced they were right. So there they were, all in their little groups, taking part in the Lord's Supper.

And isn't that just the kind of thing that goes on today? Someone in the church will take a stand on what he or she regards as a point of principle and will pray piously, "Lord, you know what these silly people round here are like: they don't know that You and I have got it right."

The divisions in the Corinthian church stemmed from the fact that the people were full of their own importance; they were convinced they were right and had to prove it. But Paul says, "I know nothing against myself." He will not even judge himself. For the day will come when God "will reveal the purposes of the hearts" (1 Cor. 4:4–5).

The second problem was that they did not worship at the Lord's Table together. Verses 20 and 21 of chapter 11 bring this out: "Therefore when you come together into one place, it is not to eat the Lord's Supper. [The Greek here reads, "It is not possible to eat the Lord's Supper."] For in eating, each one eats his own supper ahead of others. One goes hungry, and another becomes drunk." As the NIV says, "For when you are eating, some of you go ahead with your own private suppers."

In the early days of the church, the Lord's Supper took the form of a "love-feast" or common meal, which climaxed in the Communion meal as we know it. However, because of their bad behavior, the meal could not be called "the Lord's Supper." They might think it was the Lord's Supper, said Paul, but it was not. "Don't you have homes to eat and drink in?" he says (v. 22).

The third thing the Corinthians were doing wrong was that they were abusing the church by carrying their open divisions, even their class distinctions, right into the church. In verse 22 Paul asks, "Or do you despise the church of God by humiliating those who have nothing?" I wonder how many Christians today have read that passage a thousand times and never noticed the words *those who have nothing*.

These Corinthian Christians were pretending to worship. They were coming in with food, and it didn't seem to bother them that there were some who didn't have anything to eat. So Paul pleaded with them not to come into the church to parade their greed, for that only emphasized their economic divisions.

And this also applies to us. If we are divided among ourselves and eaten up by resentment and self-righteousness, then let us please stay at home and not come to the Lord's Table. Because if we do come, we will not be worshipping properly.

At this point Paul elucidates the true purpose and meaning of the Lord's Supper. He says in verses 23–25: "I have received of the Lord that which I delivered to you: that the Lord Jesus, on the night in which He was betrayed, took bread. When He had given thanks, He broke it and said, 'Take and eat. This is My body which is broken for you. Do this in remembrance of Me.' In the same manner He took the cup after He had supper, saying, 'This cup is the new covenant in My blood. Do this, as often as you drink it, in remembrance of Me.'"

Here Paul does something that he doesn't do many times in the New Testament. He brings in the fact that he got this teaching from Jesus Himself: "I have received of the Lord..."

While we know that Paul believed he got all that he said from the Lord, once in a while, for emphasis, he actually says that he did. And New Testament scholars know these vents as "the word of the Lord sayings." You can read one in 1 Thessalonians 4:15: "For this we say to you by the word of the Lord, that we who are alive and remain until the coming of the Lord will not precede those who are asleep."

Paul reserves this emphasis for very important points, which is why he uses it here. And from these verses we can discover what you might call the "ABC" of worship at the Lord's Table. For it is amazing how we can do something for years and years and think we know so much about it, only to find suddenly that we really know so little.

The first thing we can see is that worship at the Lord's Table was initiated by Jesus Christ Himself. It is the Lord's own design. So much of what we do in our church services is merely man-made tradition. In fact, one reason for this series of studies on worship is to see if we can discover what the true spiritual elements of worship are. But with the Lord's Supper there should be no confusion because, if we look carefully at the New Testament teaching, we find that God has told us all we need to know about its purpose and structure.

First, we see, for example, that the Lord's Supper need not be a very lengthy meal because there is just bread and wine. You don't come to the Lord's Table to get your stomach filled.

Second, the satisfaction we get from this table is spiritual and not physical.

Third, the meal is given in honor of Jesus Christ and not of anyone else who may be partaking. In particular it points to His death, His resurrection, and His second coming. Thus, in 1 Corinthians 11:26 Paul concludes: "As often as you eat this bread and drink this cup, you proclaim the Lord's death until He comes."

The second main thing we can see is that true worship at the Lord's Table only happens when certain conditions are in operation. Paul gives a series of sober exhortations, and whether or not we apply them will determine whether we will actually worship at the Lord's Table.

The first is that the eating and drinking be done in a worthy manner because "whoever eats this bread and drinks this cup of the Lord unworthily will be guilty of the body and blood of the Lord" (v. 27). And Paul says no more on this subject at this juncture.

The second thing which must happen is that there must be self-examination. Verse 28 says: "Let a man examine himself, and so eat of the bread and drink of the cup."

The third exhortation is that there should be a discerning of the Lord's body: "For he who eats and drinks unworthily, eats and drinks damnation to himself, not discerning the Lord's body" (v. 29).

What did Paul mean by *unworthily*? This word has been a problem for many of us because the criteria for "worthiness" can easily be misunderstood, especially by people with sensitive consciences or by the self-righteous who think they are obviously worthy.

But worthiness does not necessarily relate to our outward and moral conduct. It may, but we can be scrupulously moral and still be very unworthy. Worthiness is based upon our ability to discern the Lord's body. And that ability does not come from a high level of intelligence or an extensive theological training. It comes through self-examination (v. 28).

But what kind of "examination" is it that the worshipper must pass? And what is meant by *the Lord's body*?

First of all, the examination. This should be both subjective and objective. Paul puts the subjective examination first. When you are being subjective, you examine yourself. And Paul, in his account of the ways the Corinthians were abusing the Lord's Table, gave them the standards against which they were to examine themselves.

Now it may be that you feel these criticisms of the Corinthians don't apply to you. Certainly these are not the only ways in which the Lord's Supper can be abused. Nevertheless, if you examine yourself, you may be surprised at how relevant they are. I have been very convicted as I have prepared the material for this chapter, and I have come to the conclusion that I myself have partaken of the Lord's Supper unworthily many times and that God has been very merciful to me.

How, then, do we set about this subjective examination? Simply, we look at the criticisms Paul makes and ask ourselves honestly whether we ever do the same things. First, do I go about claiming that my particular views have God's stamp of approval? The invariable cause of divisions among the people of God is the claim to be right. You may claim that the church services ought to start at 10:30 a.m. or at 11 a.m., or that there should be more prayer meetings or more evangelism—and you may be right in your views. But you *don't* have to claim that you are. The great apostle Paul said, "I don't even judge myself" (1 Cor. 4:3). There will come a day when the secret counsels of our hearts will all be out in the open. And that will be an awful day. Then everyone will know who really had God's approval, and the more you have overclaimed, the more you will blush.

I find it quite extraordinary that Paul should say that he would not judge himself. Are we really so sure that we have God's approval? If we are, then we are claiming more even than Paul.

The second question I should ask myself is: So I take the bread and wine as if I am engaging in a private ritual between myself and Jesus alone?

Third, am I indifferent to the needs and feelings of those who are not as well off as I? Am I insensitive to others? Here were these people in the church of Corinth with their big baskets of food, and they just ate away. It didn't bother them that there were families around with very little to eat, burdened by financial worries. Instead they looked at them and said, "These people ought to get jobs. It's their own fault if they're poor. They must be doing something wrong."

James 2:6 says, "But you have despised the poor." An individual Christian or a church with that mentality is not discerning the Lord's body. When Paul wrote to the Galatian Christians, he reminded them that James, Cephas, and John (with whom he had had difficulties) all agreed with him that they "should remember the poor" (Gal. 2:10).

A church that is to have the blessing of God must be a people's church. Not a trendy church. Not a student church. Not an elitist or a middle-class body. All the kinds of people that Jesus attracted must feel welcome.

Let these three words help us then with our self-examination: self-importance, self-isolation, and insensitivity. We will have passed the test when we refuse to claim that we are in the right over against another Christian, when we are at peace with all our Christian brothers and sisters, and when we feel an abiding compassion for those who don't have as much as we have.

That is the subjective examination. When we have got this right, we will likely pass the objective examination, which is the examination that Jesus gives us when we face Him at His coming again: our hope is in His blood.

Now I want to move on to the second question I raised, which was: What is actually meant by *the Lord's body*?

Put simply, it is feeling Jesus near. It is *not* seeing physical bread and calling it Jesus. It is *not* seeing physical wine and calling it Jesus's blood. It is not even just concluding that you are saved because you are trusting in the merit of His death, although of course it includes that. But neither is it seeing the Lord's Supper merely as a memorial service. That is taking the words, "Do this in remembrance of Me," too far (1 Cor. 11:25).

Calvin got it right when he said it is "discerning His spiritual presence." When we partake of the bread and the wine, Jesus draws near. We know this because He said that He would be there. In Matthew 26:29 Jesus said, "I say to you, I will not drink of this fruit of the vine from now on until that day when I drink it new with you in My Father's kingdom." And the kingdom of Jesus is here, now. As Christians we are members of it. So when we come to the Lord's Supper, Jesus is there. The question to ask is: Do we see Him?

But why does Paul say, "The Lord's body"? It is because Jesus has a body. It wasn't only His spirit or His soul that ascended. Jesus is in His body now. The Spirit will make Him real to us to the extent that our pride is swallowed up by true humility.

But finally, what if we don't discern Him? Well, there is judgment. This is the word Paul uses, although the Authorized Version says "damnation": "For he that eateth and drinketh unworthily, eateth and drinketh damnation to himself" (1 Cor. 11:29). This refers to temporal judgment—that is, it takes place in this life. It takes two forms (there may be others, but here Paul specifies two): God can judge us (v. 32) or we can judge ourselves (v. 31). Its purpose is that we should not be condemned along with the world in the final judgment (v. 32). We know this will not happen to Christians—the Lord shows that Christians are His children by judging them Himself and chastening them in this life (v. 32).

This chastening is described in verse 30: "For this reason many are weak and unhealthy among you, and many die." Because these people in Corinth had abused the Lord's Supper by violating the three principles I have shown you, some of them had become ill, and some had actually died. This was God's judgment on them.

Alternatively, we can judge ourselves in the ways I have shown you in this chapter. Then God will say: "All right, thank you for that. Now I won't have to judge you." "If we would judge ourselves, we would not be judged" (v. 31). If we confess our sins to God, we relieve Him of having to judge us. He doesn't want to step in, for if He does, it may not be so pleasant. But "if we confess our sins, He is faithful and just to forgive us our sins and cleanse us from all unrighteousness." (1 John 1:9).

And when we are cleansed, the ungrieved Spirit manifests Himself—the Lord is among us—and we worship as we meet with Him at His Table.

CHAPTER 10

THE CHURCH AT PRAYER

*They continued steadfastly in the apostles' teaching and
fellowship, in the breaking of bread and in the prayers.*

—ACTS 2:42

PRAYER CAN NO more be divorced from worship than life
can be divorced from breathing. If we follow His impulse,
the Holy Spirit will always lead us to pray. When we
allow Him to work freely, He will always bring the church to
extensive praying. Conversely, when the Spirit is absent, we
will find excuses not to pray. We may say, "God understands.
He knows I love Him. But I'm tired. I'm so busy. It's just not
convenient now…" When the Spirit is absent, our excuses
always seem right, but in the presence of the Spirit our excuses
fade away.

All prayer comes from the Spirit—be it disciplined prayer or
spontaneous prayer.

We pray spontaneously, both privately and with other
Christians, when we are suddenly aware of a great need in the
world or the church. There are two examples of this in Acts. In
chapter 12 we are told that Herod had just killed James, the
brother of John, and had thrown Peter in prison. The church
was wondering just what would happen next, and we read in
verse 5: "So Peter was kept in prison. But the church prayed
to God without ceasing for him." This was spontaneous prayer
caused by a burden for Peter.

The other example is in the passage in Acts 4 that we looked
at in Chapter 8. Peter and John had been called before the

Sanhedrin and had been commanded "not to speak or teach at all in the name of Jesus" (v. 18). And when they reported this to the church, a burden came on the people so that "when they heard this, they lifted their voices in unity to God and prayed... 'Now, Lord, look on their threats'" (vv. 24, 29).

God often uses something external to bring the church to her knees. We ought to see it as the kindness of God when He allows trouble to drive us to prayer. In our individual lives, family tension or financial worries or illness will do it. With the church it can be threats—"look on their threats..."—or fear of the future. The early church did not know what they would do without Peter.

We also pray spontaneously when there is an overwhelming inner pressure from the Spirit resulting in a vivid awareness of the Spirit's presence. When this happens within the church, people come from everywhere to be there. You've heard of the moral majority, and the silent majority. Here I'm talking about the sudden majority!

I've already written about the great outpouring of the Spirit that is taking place in South Korea. The largest church in the world is in Seoul. Hundreds of people come every morning at five o'clock to pray before they go to work. Just imagine doing that! Yet this is what will likely happen in our churches when the ungrieved Spirit is present in power.

The people who appear from nowhere and get involved in praying will not have been toiling in prayer for months, even years, seeking God for this very outpouring of the Spirit. Yet they will derive as much benefit, if not more, as those who have been bearing the burden of prayer, and this can be a source of tension. There will be a temptation to bitterness when the faithful few see outsiders take the limelight and receive such great blessing. Do you remember the parable which Jesus told in Matthew 20 about the manager of the vineyard who hired some laborers to work all day for a penny? We are told that at the eleventh hour he found some more men who didn't have anything to do, and he hired them also to work for a penny.

But when the wages were given out, those who had worked all day supposed that they would get more than the men who had come in at the eleventh hour, and they were very angry when they didn't. Well, this is what will happen when the Spirit comes. Others will come in at "the eleventh hour" and will be blessed. As Jesus said, "But many who are first will be last, and the last first" (Matt. 19:30).

What are the characteristics of this kind of spontaneous impulse to pray? There are four: time becomes unimportant; there is a caring for others (for example, in Acts 2:44 we are told that the believers "had all things in common"); there is clear guidance; and there is unity (Acts 2:46 in the KJV says there was "singleness of heart").

The result of all this is—worship. We need to understand that worship is not just singing hymns, nor even consciously adoring God. Some people think that worship is limited to the moments in which one is saying, "God, I worship You." But this is a wrong idea. Worship is any activity which is carried out under the impulse of the Spirit of God, and we are also worshipping God when we are praying for others or witnessing to others.

Arthur Blessitt tells of a church that decided to meet on a Saturday afternoon to pray for revival. About forty men came, sat in a big circle, and started to pray. The first man prayed for about five to six minutes in pious tones, with all the right phrases. The second did the same, and the third, the fourth, and the fifth. But there was no sense of the presence of God. Arthur groaned to himself and thought, "There's something wrong here."

At that moment he happened to look out of the window, and he noticed a restaurant across the street. He felt an impulse to get up and go over there, so he did. He stood inside the door and said, as only Arthur could say, "Does anybody here want to get saved?"

A waitress immediately said, "I do."

So he went over to her, explained the gospel, and led her to the Lord.

Then he asked her how long she had been working in the restaurant, and she said, "Two years."

He asked her if she knew any of the people from the church across the street, and she replied, "Oh, yes, they come here all the time, especially after the Sunday morning service."

So he asked her if any of these people had ever talked to her about Jesus Christ or invited her to come to church.

She said, "No, not a one."

Yet those same people were praying for revival.

Arthur walked back into the prayer meeting (where they had reached about the eighteenth person) and said to them, "You can stop your praying. God has shown us what to do."

Do not limit the Spirit by presuming that your familiar, comfortable pattern of worship is the pattern He wants. Those forty men ended up praying more than ever—but first they had to be dislodged from their deadness. Worship and prayer under the impulse of the Spirit means following the Spirit.

So far I have just been speaking about spontaneous prayer. There is also what I call the disciplined impulse, the trained impulse to pray. I think this is what we particularly need to hear about today. Hebrews 5:14 says, "But solid food belongs to those who are mature, for those who through practice have powers of discernment that are trained to distinguish good from evil." The disciplined impulse is a developed sense of what pleases God. It is true spirituality,

Disciplined prayer arises from two things: first, a good general knowledge of God's Word, and second, a strong desire to please Him. In other words, I am talking here about praying as an act of sheer obedience whether we feel like it or not. And it is the mature Christian who follows this way. If you think that the spontaneous impulse is the only kind that matters, you show yourself to be a superficial Christian. If you only respond to God when you are carried along by feeling, then you are an immature Christian.

Paul said to Timothy, "Be ready in season and out of season" (2 Tim. 4:2). There are times when the spontaneous impulse is at work: this corresponds to being "in season." There are also times when we feel nothing: this is being "out of season." It is what the members of a church do when they are "out of season" that testifies to their maturity. And it is this that demonstrates their commitment to God and each other.

Someone came to see me who said that, as a result of reading one of my books, he had started to tithe. "But," he said, "ever since I started, I've had nothing but financial trouble. So I guess the Holy Spirit is telling me not to tithe." But his problem was that he was not committed. When God leads us to do something, we have got to do it.

You may decide to spend more time in prayer, but then you find that everything seems to militate against it. So you think, "These things which are stopping me praying are providential."

That's what Jonah said. He ran from God and wanted to get a ship to Tarshish. Lo and behold—when he got to the dock, there was a ship going to Tarshish! And he said to himself, "This is providential." We can call any sin or temptation providential.

So don't be surprised if, when you commit yourself to prayer, everything seems to be hindering you. There must be discipline. If you live only by the spontaneous impulse to pray, you will become like the Quakers, who carry the idea of being led by the Spirit to extremes. I heard of a couple who waited for two hours for the man who was to marry them to feel moved by the Spirit to perform the ceremony. And they eventually left in tears because he never did feel moved.

One of the forgotten verses in the Book of Acts is the opening verse of chapter 3. The chapter goes on to describe how Peter and John healed the crippled man, but what is interesting is that it happened when they were on their way to the temple to pray. Verse 1 says, "Now Peter and John went up together to the temple at the ninth hour, *the hour of prayer*" (emphasis added). This was three o'clock in the afternoon. So we see that even when the Spirit was present in great power, these early disciples were not afraid to go by a schedule. At this high peak in the history of the church it would seem that the first Christians still observed set times for prayer.

The principle is that, if you live by the disciplined impulse, you will get the spontaneous impulse as well, and this is why I urge each Christian to pray for thirty minutes a day and to attend the weekly church prayer meetings. Here were Peter and John on their way to the temple, when the lame beggar held out his hand to them, expecting to receive some money. But Peter just turned to him and said, "I have no silver and gold, but I give you what I have. In the name of Jesus Christ of Nazareth, rise up and walk" (Acts 3:6). And the man was healed.

At the end of Luke's Gospel we are told that Jesus appeared to "the eleven and those who were with them assembled together" (Luke 24:33), and said, "But wait in the city of Jerusalem until you are clothed with power from on high" (v. 49). On the day of Pentecost one hundred twenty people were present, and in only ten days that comparatively small number of one hundred twenty praying people gathered out of contemporary Judaism a Christian congregation of three thousand. What occurred in Acts chapter 1 was done by disciplined impulse: "These all continued with one accord in prayer and supplication" (v. 14). What took place in Acts 2 was by spontaneous impulse: "And they were all filled with the Holy Spirit and began to speak in other tongues, as the Spirit enabled them to speak" (v. 4). And what followed? "They continued steadfastly in the apostles' teaching and fellowship, in the breaking of bread and in the *prayers*" (v. 42, emphasis added). You never outgrow the need to pray.

One May evening, while I was going through my reading for the day, I came across Psalm 50:12, where God says, "If I were hungry, I would not tell you." And something happened to me then. That verse did more to convict me to pray than any book on prayer I have read. You may think that it has nothing to do with prayer, but this verse showed me that God will not necessarily tell us when we are doing it wrong. We may justify ourselves when we don't have time to pray, and our reasons may sound perfectly good and right to us. But God has said, "If I were hungry, I would not tell you." None of us is so spiritual that we can assume that God will tap us on the shoulder and let us know every time we are doing it wrong. This convinced me that it is my job, not only as a Christian minister but as a child of God, never to excuse myself again for what I haven't done regarding time spent in prayer.

A lot of the praying I've been talking about in this chapter is not going to take place on Sundays, but on other days of the week, when we are by ourselves or in small groups. I long for the Christian church to give more time to disciplined prayer. It is not always exciting, but without it there will be no spiritual life and no worship of any kind.

CHAPTER 11

LIFESTYLE WORSHIP

*I, therefore, the prisoner of the Lord, exhort
you to walk in a manner worthy of the
calling with which you were called.*

—EPHESIANS 4:1

IN THESE PAST chapters we have seen that worship is not a performance or an ego trip. It is something that glorifies God and pleases Him. God tells us how to worship Him, and we find out, not by looking over our shoulder at what other people are doing, not by following trends, be they charismatic or anti-charismatic, but by faithful prayer and by listening to God's Word in expectancy and humility.

We have also seen that worship does not only happen on a Sunday in church, but whenever we act in obedience to the impulse of the Spirit and in His power. If an ungrieved Spirit is at work in us, we will be worshipping in all we do, and we will get worship right.

This is something I want to look at more closely. What we are individually, twenty-four hours a day, is more important than what happens in church once a week. The secret of acceptable worship lies in how we are at home or at work, and when we are alone and nobody knows what we are doing. It lies in our total lifestyle. Jesus said, "He who is faithful in what is least is faithful also in much" (Luke 16:10). If we don't get our act together before we come to church, we can't expect to worship at church. We can't expect something magical to happen once we're inside the church doors. We mustn't think, "All I need to do is get to church," because it doesn't work that way. If we are hypocrites, if our profession of faith lacks reality, when we come to church to sing and worship, we will be out of tune and will not be making music pleasing to God.

In our corporate worship it is essential to have inner—spiritual—harmony. In Ephesians 4:3 Paul speaks of "the unity of the Spirit." By this he means that the leadership of the Spirit in you will not contradict the leadership of the Spirit in me. If we are guided by the Spirit, we will be in agreement. The ungrieved Spirit in me can detect the ungrieved Spirit in you, and there will be no heaviness when we come together—only peace and agreement.

Matthew 18:19 says, "If two of you agree on earth about anything they ask, it will be done for them by My Father who is in heaven." This word that is translated *agree* is the Greek word from which we also get the word *symphony*. It is used like this in Acts 15:15: "With this the words of the prophets agree." In Acts 5:9 it is said of Ananias and Sapphira: "How is it that you have agreed together to test the Spirit of the Lord?" 2 Corinthians 6:15 (KJV) translates it as *concord*: "What concord hath Christ with Belial?"

In a symphony orchestra all the instruments play their own parts but according to one overall pattern, and the result is lovely music. But how did the individuals in an orchestra learn to play their instruments? If I suddenly wanted an orchestra here today and passed out instruments among you all, would you know what to do with them?

I was an oboist in a symphony orchestra when I was in high school in Kentucky. I learned that when the conductor comes up with a piece, he wants each member to practice it during the week. So I had to take the score home with me. And how well the orchestra performed at the next rehearsal depended on how each person handled his own part.

It is the same with worship. It is not possible, for example, to go to Hyde Park Corner and say, "I want a hundred people to stand over here—it doesn't matter whether you are a Christian or not—and we are all going to worship God." You just don't do it like that. When we meet together to worship, God is not looking for aesthetic beauty but for the presence of the ungrieved Spirit in each worshipping member of the congregation.

It is said that the great conductor Arturo Toscanini had such a perfect ear that he could detect if the fifth violinist on the fourth row back was slightly out of tune. Well, I don't know if it is possible for any minister to have that kind of sensitivity about his congregation. But God knows when there is perfect harmony and a lifestyle that is in accord with the Spirit—and He is not to be fooled or played around with.

The way we guard against being a hypocrite six days a week and acting piously on Sundays is by applying the Word of God to our lives. Revival in a church may be quite extraordinary, but it is only a question of whether each member is following the conductor's score in his private life. In an orchestra the sound is no greater than the sum of the different parts. As Paul says in Ephesians 4:16: "From whom the whole body is joined together and connected by every joint and ligament, as every part effectively does its work and grows, building itself up in love." So our worship ought to be a glorious symphony to God—no one out of tune, no one playing too loudly, each person following his or her own score.

Though our worship is not a performance designed to attract other people or pander to our own love of display, there is a sense in which it is a performance—a performance for God. I don't know what it would be like to play for Her Majesty the Queen—but I know it is considered a great honor. If she were to go to a concert in the Royal Albert Hall, the orchestra would certainly want to play very well that day. Our worship is for God, the King of kings—should that not affect us as we prepare for the Sunday worship since our Sunday worship is the culmination of what we are all the time?

How do we actually achieve this? How does the right performance come about? There are several ways, and as I've indicated, the first is practice at the individual level. I don't mean that we spend the week rehearsing the following Sunday's hymns! Paul says in Ephesians 4:1–2: "I, therefore, the prisoner of the Lord, exhort you to walk in a manner worthy of the calling with which you were called. With all humility, meekness, and patience, bearing with one another in love." This is what we must do—and practice makes perfect!

Brother Lawrence, the French monk, says in his book, *The Practice of the Presence of God*, that he felt the presence of the Lord as much among the rattling of the pots and pans in the monastery kitchen where he washed up as when he was "upon [his] knees at the Blessed Sacrament."[1] He knew the presence of God all the time. We can all practice living in the presence of God from minute to minute. And in order to do this, we must outlaw all bitterness from our lives. We must seek to be filled with love and with total forgiveness and acceptance of each other.

The second way a correct performance in worship is achieved is when we all discover our place in the great orchestra. Ephesians 4:7 says, "But grace was given to each one of us according to the measure of the gift of Christ." Of course, there is a difference between being in an orchestra and finding our place in the body of Christ, because in an orchestra we are the ones who choose the instrument we are going to play, but with the body God selects our part.

The question of spiritual gifts is a subject of great importance, and I wish to spend the next chapter considering it. However, I would like to give two general principles here, for if followed, they will both have a dramatic effect on our lifestyle and go a long way to resolving the difficulties so many Christians have with this subject.

Do you wish to discover your spiritual gift? Two passages in particular tell you how to do it.

In 1 Corinthians 12:31 Paul says, "But earnestly covet the greater gifts. Yet I show you a more excellent way." In the Greek this passage means "The excellent *way by which you discover* your gifts is by love." It sounds almost too simple to be true: you can best discover your gift when you demonstrate agape love. Yet it is true. When we love people and long to serve them, when we totally forgive and keep no record of wrongs, then we spontaneously find ways of expressing that love, and the gifts of the Spirit emerge in us. There are no shortcuts to finding the gifts. We must have hearts devoid of bitterness.

The second principle is found in Romans 12. Paul says here: "I urge you therefore, brothers, by the mercies of God, that you present your bodies as a living sacrifice, holy, and acceptable to God, which is your reasonable service of worship. Do not be conformed to this world, but be transformed by the renewing of your mind, that you may prove what is the good and acceptable and perfect will of God" (vv. 1–2).

He goes on to add: "For I say, through the grace given to me, to everyone among you, not to think of himself more highly than he ought to think, but to think with sound judgment, according to the measure of faith God has distributed to every man" (v. 3). Paul means: don't claim to have what you don't have.

Though, as we will see in the next chapter, we are to covet the gifts, we must not seek them for our own glory or impute to ourselves abilities that simply aren't there. Our lives must be given over to the praise and love of God. We must live sacrificial lives, seeking at each moment only to love and serve God in holiness, humility, and prayer. Then, though we may not be the first violinist or the conductor, we will quite naturally and simply find our own gift, and our place in the orchestra, almost without realizing it. Sometimes we may find we are merely sweeping up; sometimes the position may be quite prominent. But it will be under God's control and God's responsibility, and almost a matter of indifference to us since all that matters is God's glory and not ours. "But are you seeking great things for yourself? Do not seek them," said Jeremiah (45:5).

One further guideline here is that God does not encourage us to be incompetent, and if we feel that we are working incompetently, then it is a pretty strong hint that we are not where God intended us to be. We have gotten there by ourselves. And the indication that something is not right is that we will have stress and worry and fatigue. If you find that these are the marks of your life, ask God what He wants you to change in your life, and then offer yourself to Him again as a living and daily sacrifice.

Then the third way to achieve a right performance is to accept God's verdict concerning the conductor. Ephesians 4:11 says that God "gave some to be apostles, prophets, evangelists, pastors, and teachers." Your minister has been called by God to his present work. It is a task of the utmost responsibility. We have already considered the role of preaching in worship, and I shall be going on in Chapter 13 to look at the gift of leadership. An orchestra is not better than its conductor, so if the worship of a church isn't pleasing to God, there is a sense in which the blame falls on the vicar, pastor, or elder. If a congregation takes his teaching seriously and tries to follow it, and then finds it doesn't work and their soul is starved and God's Spirit is grieved, then he must be responsible.

However, the congregation must pray for their minister and seek to follow and respect his teaching. The writer to the Hebrews says, "Remember those who rule over you, who have proclaimed to you the word of God. Follow their faith, considering the results it has produced in their lives" (Heb. 13:7). And you can't do this for just an hour or two on a Sunday—it is a daily obedience and respect or it is nothing at all. For there is also a sense in which the conductor is no greater than the members of his congregation. There is a limit to what he can do, and he cannot lead unless his congregation is willing to follow him.

This takes us on to the next point: the fourth way to find the right performance is to see that the whole orchestra follows the same score. If, when the conductor announces that the music is from Mozart, the first violinist says, "I don't feel led to play Mozart today—I'm going to play Beethoven!" or the French horn player says, "I'm going to play Rachmaninoff," and the trumpeter says, "I'm into Schumann today..." it will sound rather ridiculous when the conductor starts to wave his baton.

We do not have the right merely to do our own thing. We must follow the truth, which means the Holy Scriptures. A conductor interprets the score, and a minister interprets the Scriptures. That is his job. And it is our job to follow the score and to be governed by the teaching of the Bible each day of the week.

The mark that we are getting it right in our churches is when we see the members of the congregation growing together into maturity and Christ-likeness... Ephesians 4:13 says: "Until we all come into the unity of the faith and of the knowledge of the Son of God, into a complete man, to the measure of the stature of the fullness of Christ."

We will also find that there is increasing stability in our churches: "So we may no longer be children, tossed here and there by waves and carried about with every wind of doctrine by the trickery of men, by craftiness with deceitful scheming" (Eph. 4:14). If truth is recognized from error, if the church members are not swayed by fashions and gimmicks—then they are worshipping by the impulse of the Spirit.

And the result will be harmony: the whole body fitly joined together. When God's people are living lives of worship; when they know their part in God's body; when no one is out of tune and there is no bitterness; when no one is trying to get attention by playing too loudly and everyone is following the Word of God and the leadership God has provided—then a great symphony of worship ascends to God, the world outside marvels, and new members are added to the church.

CHAPTER 12

SPIRITUAL GIFTS AND WORSHIP

We have diverse gifts according to
the grace that is given to us.

—ROMANS 12:6

WE ARE ALL aware that there is widespread interest in the subject of the gifts of the Spirit. Paul devotes considerable space to spiritual gifts and does so in the context of worship. I myself covet all the spiritual gifts for myself and each member of my congregation. In fact, the only justifiable covetousness in the Bible is with reference to the gifts of the Spirit! In 1 Corinthians 12:31, Paul says, "But earnestly covet the greater gifts." God has given us carte blanche to come before Him and ask for the gifts of the Spirit.

There is not one shred of biblical evidence that the gifts of the Spirit ceased in the early church just because we now have the Bible, though this is the view of some godly people. With the deepest respect, I maintain that this is simply a theological cop-out by those who want to explain the absence of supernatural power in the church today. Those who hold this view support their argument with 1 Corinthians 13:10: "But when that which is perfect comes, then that which is imperfect shall pass away." But when Paul talks of "that which is perfect," he is not referring to the Bible but to love. He has just said, "Love never fails. But if there are prophecies, they shall fail; if there are tongues, they shall cease; and if there is knowledge, it shall vanish" (v. 8). And in verse 10 he is showing that the gifts of the Spirit may subside, but love goes on.

All the spiritual gifts described in 1 Corinthians 12:8–10 are available today should God be pleased to grant them. The attainment of a spiritual gift ought not to be any more unusual than the attainment of love. It is clearly our responsibility today to seek the gift of love—and it is equally our responsibility to seek the gifts of the Spirit. As we pray for revival, which continues to tarry, so ought we to pray for the gifts of the Spirit. That we may not have them does not mean that we cannot have them any more than the absence of revival proves that revival will never come.

I personally doubt that the possession of supernatural gifts is common in the western church today. It may be that in third world countries spiritual gifts are more frequent. I think that there is some merit to unusual claims that come from the third world, but I don't think the gifts are widespread in Britain, even though many people are claiming to have them. Most claims to the miraculous in Britain do not stand the test of scrutiny. And why believe the claims regarding the unverifiable gifts, such as the word of knowledge, prophecy, and tongues, when the so-called miracles usually appear phony when you examine them seriously?

Is it possible that many people are attracted to the gift of tongues because they can be imitated if you try hard enough and it's not easy to verify them? In a charismatic church in London people stayed behind for open worship after the service. A man was present who felt he would like to pray. When everyone heard him pray, they took it to be an unknown tongue, and the curate, who was in the chair, gave the interpretation with words to this effect: "Someone here is getting his last warning. You had better act. God is speaking to someone here and you had better obey." The man who prayed the prayer just got up and walked out. He was an African and had been praying in his own language, thanking God for His goodness and mercy.

There is, however, one test that we can apply to gifts of the

Spirit within a church in order to verify whether or not they are genuinely from God or just imitations. The clue is given in 1 Corinthians 14:22–25. Paul says, "So tongues are for a sign, not to believers, but to unbelievers. But prophesying does not serve unbelievers, but believers. Therefore if the whole church assembles in one place and all speak with tongues, and those who are unlearned or unbelievers come in, will they not say that you are out of your mind? But if all prophesy and there comes in one who does not believe or one unlearned, he is convinced by all and judged by all. Thus the secrets of his heart are revealed. And so falling down on his face, he will worship God and report that God is truly among you."

When the gifts of prophecy and tongues are used in a church, they result in conversions. When Jesus performed miracles, He would say, "Go to the priest; let him see you. Let him see that you are no longer a leper." There was no need to overclaim and pretend. The real gifts of the Spirit will mean that the miracles will be undoubted; the healings will be undoubted—and people will be converted.

In saying this, I am trying to be as honest as I can. I do not think one can follow on from this point and say, "I just don't believe the gifts are available." That is an ostrich-like approach. We may not be seeing the real gifts at the moment, but this should not discourage us. We believe the Bible, which is God's infallible Word, and God says, "Earnestly covet the best gifts" (1 Cor. 12:31). Am I to believe that this command does not apply to me? "Jesus Christ is the same yesterday, and today, and forever" (Heb. 13:8). There is nothing to stop Him pouring out the Spirit of God in great measure should He want to do so.

We have three options. One is to forget all about the gifts of the Spirit. Another is to claim that they are everywhere, as many charismatics maintain. The third is simply to wait for the authentic gifts. That is the option I take.

I have three main observations to make based upon 1 Corinthians 12–14. The first is this: even when the gifts are undoubtedly being exercised, not all Christians have them, for

Paul says, "The body is not one part, but many. If the foot says, 'Because I am not the hand, I am not of the body,' is it therefore not of the body? And if the ear says, 'Because I am not the eye, I am not of the body,' is it therefore not of the body? If the whole body were an eye, where would the hearing be? If the whole body were hearing, where would the sense of smell be? But now God has established the parts, every one of them, in the body as it has pleased Him" (1 Cor. 12:14–18). We all have different gifts, and every gift that God has tapped us on the shoulder and given us is equally important in the body.

In our physical body, if we have a sore toe, we will be miserable all day long. We can go to the doctor with an ingrown toenail and be waiting there with someone who has cancer and someone else with a terrible heart disease. When our turn comes and the doctor says, "What's the matter with you?" and we say, "I've got an ingrown toenail," we may feel stupid. We may feel we shouldn't have gone to the doctor with something so small. Yet an ingrown toenail can cause terrific pain. The smallest part of the body can affect the whole.

When we get to heaven, the recognition there will not match earthly recognition. In heaven that one who is the little toe in the body will be rewarded as much as the eye if he has been faithful in that task.

My second observation from these chapters is that, even though we are encouraged to covet any true gift of the Spirit, any gift given will be by the sovereign will of God.

"But that one and very same Spirit works all these, dividing to each one individually as He will" (1 Cor. 12:11). Look at verse 18: "But now God has established the parts, every one of them, in the body as it has pleased Him." When it comes to the gifts of the Spirit, whether we like it or not, we are shut up to the sovereignty of God. Consequently, we must beware of the danger of working ourselves up and producing the unauthentic and phony.

Would you want God to do what He doesn't want to do? Would you want to have what God doesn't want you to have?

Think of verse 15 in Psalm 106: "He gave them their request, but He sent a wasting disease on them." I don't want to be found trusting God for anything but what He wants to give to me.

When God gives a gift of the Spirit, it is for two reasons. The first is for His glory. We must ask ourselves what our motive is for wanting a gift of the Spirit. What is our motive for wanting to see healings? It may be that we want to get a bit of glory for ourselves. In that case God knows that we couldn't be trusted with these gifts. How dare we want to compete with God's glory! May we be brought to the place where we are so totally dedicated to His honor and glory that God can trust us with the unusual. The withholding of God's gifts suggests that our motives are wrong.

The second reason He gives a gift is for the edification of others: "So, seeing that you are zealous of spiritual gifts, seek that you may excel to the edifying of the church" (1 Cor. 14:12). God gives gifts so that we may be givers.

Do you know what may well be the greatest gift of the Spirit? It is described in 1 Corinthians 12. Most of us have heard of the gifts of knowledge, of faith, of miracles, of tongues. We have heard of the gift of the interpretation of tongues. But how many know about the gifts of *helps*? "God has put these in the church: first apostles, second prophets, third teachers, after that miracles, then gifts of healings, helps..." (v. 28).

Someone may say, "Help! I've only got the gift of helps!" Maybe your church needs cleaning and you are the one gifted to do it. Or somebody is needed to help in the kitchen. Stewards, musicians, typists, Sunday school helpers, people who go out witnessing, or help run meetings and organizations, consistent tithers—these people should be doing this work with the God-given gift of help. Some can only do one thing. Some can do three or four things without fatigue. The body will never be tired and no one will be overworked when we all do our part. If someone is the little toe and works well, that person will see that the body goes on without any pain.

A man may be praying for the gift of healing and be blind to the fact that he has a gift—to help, make coffee. How sad for him that he doesn't see it. Maybe by ignoring this gift, he is blocking the way for the gift of healing.

As far as I am able to tell, spiritual gifts emerge in one of two ways. First, it may be your natural gift plus the Spirit. God had a purpose in making each of us as we are. We are each unique and each have a place in His kingdom. What we can do naturally, that is, what we would have even if we hadn't been converted, can be improved and controlled by the Spirit.

Second, there are the supernatural gifts of the Spirit such as miracles and healing. We aren't born with these gifts. To perform a miracle, to heal, is something God does. But it wouldn't surprise me for one minute if God were graciously to overrule so that the one who does the cleaning or catering is also the one who is able to lay hands on somebody and see a supernatural healing, or be given a special gift of prayer and discernment.

My third observation about 1 Corinthians 12 and 14 is that Paul gives clear instructions about how to go about obtaining the gifts. I have already touched on this in Chapter 11, but I would like to return to it. I found it thrilling when I first understood that when Paul said in 1 Corinthians 12:31: "But earnestly covet the greater gifts. Yet I show you a more excellent way," Paul was showing us *how to get the gifts.* The way to get them is by the love of 1 Corinthians 13.

One of the treasured moments of my life came some years ago when I went to Holland and was given the very high privilege of meeting Corrie ten Boom in her home. I asked her, "Is it true that you believe in all the gifts of the Spirit?"

"Oh, yes," she said. "1 Corinthians 12, 1 Corinthians 14, but don't forget 1 Corinthians 13."

Paul is saying, "The Spirit is released to be Himself to the degree that we have *agape* love." It is not by fantasizing about the gifts. It is not even by praying for them, much less coveting them. Here is the way: it is by love. The bridge that crosses the gap between the sovereignty of God and the obtaining of spiritual gifts is love.

Those of us who long for the gifts of the Spirit for our own lives and for our church worship—not the phony gifts, not the counterfeits, but the true gifts—need to apply ourselves to a number of principles from 1 Corinthians 13.

First, the love of 1 Corinthians 13 tolerates those who seem inferior. Paul says, "Love suffers long and is kind" (v. 4). They may seem inferior socially, culturally, or intellectually. They may seem inferior spiritually. But you are kind and you suffer them long.

Second, this love is content with the present circumstances. Paul says, "Love envies not" (v. 4). This is very important. James said that we should be "perfect and complete, lacking nothing" (James 1:4). "The LORD is my shepherd; I shall not want," says David (Ps. 23:1). We must come to the place where we say, "I have all that God wants me to have materially right now." Love does not envy.

Third, love doesn't want to make another person jealous. Paul says, "love flaunts not itself and is not puffed up" (1 Cor. 13:4). That means it doesn't boast. Do you know why people boast? It is partly because of their insecurity, but it is mainly because they want to be admired. At bottom, they want to make you just a bit jealous by revealing who they know, what they know, or what they have. But love protects another person from being envious.

The fourth thing is that this love is never rude: love "does not behave itself improperly" (v. 5). Fifth, love doesn't manipulate either people or progress. Paul says that it "seeks not its own" (v. 5). The NIV puts it "not self-seeking." Sixth, it doesn't exhibit a quick temper: "is not easily provoked" (v. 5). When this love sees any form of bitterness emerging on the horizon, it just refuses to give place to the devil. It also "thinks no evil" (v. 5) or "keeps no record of wrongs" (NIV). That is the way God forgives us. The blood of Jesus washes away all our sins. It is as though we never committed them. That is what love is. Paul says we should be "forgiving each other, just as in Christ God forgave you" (Eph. 4:32). If a person has hurt us, or walked over us, or been unkind to us, we don't even know about it.

All this is pretty hard. Do we want the gifts of the Spirit or have we changed our minds? Today there is an absence of the gifts of the Spirit in the church, not because they ceased with the early church, but because we all want shortcuts. Paul says, "But earnestly covet the greater gifts" (1 Cor. 12:31), and here is how to get them. We have forgotten 1 Corinthians 13, and that is why revival tarries, and there is so much that is phony.

If a man or woman came to know this kind of love, which keeps no record of wrong, knows no bitterness, doesn't want to make another person envious, isn't proud, tolerates others, and is gracious and kind and doesn't envy, it may be that he or she will wake up one day and find that God has entrusted him or her with a valuable gift that is more precious than the knowledge of a brain surgeon or the skill of the cleverest lawyer in the city. Such a person may say, "I can't believe it would happen to me.

But God has done this because love bridges the gap between the sovereignty of God and the obtaining of the gifts. How dare we talk about the gifts and treat love with contempt! If this love were to flow among us, who knows what God might do?

CHAPTER 13

LEADERSHIP IN WORSHIP

Looking upon Jesus as He walked, [John]
said, "Look, the Lamb of God!"

—JOHN 1:36

IN THIS CHAPTER I would like to concentrate on one particular and vital gift of the Spirit—the gift of leadership. From
earliest times people have needed leadership because most
people are followers. And it is no disgrace to be a follower: we
are all followers of Jesus. Those who are upset because they are
not called to be leaders in the church are criticizing the way
God made them. Everybody can be a leader in some area, but
once outside their area, they must have the grace to become followers again.

It is a sad day when God hides His face from the church and
does not raise up strong leadership. For when that happens, you
have a lot of small men scrambling for power, and it is a pitiful
sight. I don't understand why God sometimes does not provide
strong leaders—why many generations have suffered because of
this problem. One of the curious quirks (if I may put it like
this) in church history is the story of George Whitefield and
John Wesley. Here were two great men, but only one of them
was a leader. Whitefield was given over entirely to preaching,
and Wesley was the leader of men. Wesley organized many of
Whitefield's converts, and Methodism took a certain theological complexion because of Wesley's influence.

In the Welsh Revival there was no equivalent to John Wesley.
The name Evan Roberts is associated with the revival, but he

was no leader. No real leadership or definite theological direction emerged from the Welsh Revival so that, although the churches were filled for a while, when it was over, all that was left were memories.

And many churches today flounder as a consequence of an absence of able leadership. This is a day when the so-called "one-man ministry" is severely criticized. But I have long had a suspicion that the modern craze for "plurality of elders," as it is termed, has its base, not in the fact that suddenly everyone has seen the light on the teaching of elders, but in a lack of leadership. And so this practice has largely come in to fill the vacuum.

Any era where God does not raise up strong leadership is tragic. If you want to know what the Book of Judges is all about, look at its very last verse: "In those days there was no king in Israel; everyone did what was right in his own eyes" (21:25).

Moses, the greatest leader of men that ever was, had a successor in Joshua. But no one succeeded Joshua. Elijah's mantle fell on Elisha, but Elisha had no successor. And I don't understand this.

One of the main tasks of a leader in the church is to lead the worship. Obviously a leader has other responsibilities too. He must be an administrator and be able to delegate authority to those who respect him enough to follow him. He must be able to give direction and set the pace spiritually and theologically— "Where there is no vision, the people perish" (Prov. 29:18).

However, since in this book my subject is worship, I should like to concentrate on leadership in worship. It could be said that Moses's main calling was to lead worship. God came to him and said: "They shall listen to your voice, and you shall come, you and the elders of Israel, to the king of Egypt, and you must say to him, 'The Lord, the God of the Hebrews has met with us. Therefore, now, let us go, we ask you, three days' journey into the wilderness so that we may sacrifice to the Lord our God'" (Exod. 3:18).

This theme comes up again and again. Exodus 7:16 says: "The Lord, the God of the Hebrews, has sent me to you, saying,

'Let My people go, so that they may serve Me in the wilderness.'" The NIV translates it, "That they may worship me in the wilderness." Exodus 8:1 has the Lord saying to Moses, "Go to Pharaoh and say to him, 'Thus says the LORD: Let My people go, so that they may serve Me.'"

Moses was raised up to lead the people to worship God. By *lead worship* I don't just mean "conduct worship," for it doesn't take a lot to do that. I fear that there are probably hundreds of unregenerate men "conducting worship" today. What I mean by *lead worship* is lead the congregation to worship and adore God.

There are two important things to remember about leadership in worship. The first is that the leader himself must get out of the way. The best example of someone who did this is not Moses, or Samuel, or King David—who can certainly teach us a lot about leadership in worship. It isn't even the apostle Paul. It is John the Baptist.

We know that John was called by God to be a leader. He was filled with the Holy Spirit from his mother's womb. He was part of God's plan. Matthew 3:3 says:

> For this is he who was spoken of by the prophet Isaiah, saying: "The voice of one crying in the wilderness: 'Prepare the way of the Lord; make His paths straight.'"

God trained and prepared John for leadership. It is easy to forget that John the Baptist was the son of a priest. When you think of John, you get the image almost of a wild man in the desert. But he was brought up in the cultured home of a priest, and he would have known all about the ritual of worship in Israel.

God also protected and guided him. We know that John was "in the wilderness until the day of his appearance to Israel" (Luke 1:80). He stayed put until his time had come.

John's was a preaching leadership—"In those days John the Baptist came, preaching in the wilderness of Judea" (Matt. 3:1). His preaching was passionate: "But when he saw many of the

Pharisees and Sadducees come to his baptism, he said to them, 'O generation of vipers, who has warned you to escape from the wrath to come?'" (Matt. 3:7). Imagine calling these members of his congregation snakes!

But his preaching was also practical and down-to-earth: "Therefore, bear fruit worthy of repentance" (Matt. 3:8). And it was popular: "Then Jerusalem, and all Judea, and all the region around the Jordan went out to him" (Matt. 3:5). It was also effective: "and were baptized by him in the Jordan, confessing their sins" (Matt. 3:6).

Finally, his leadership was prescribed. He was a leader under authority. John didn't arbitrarily decide what to say: he was following a script. God told him what to say. And his major task was to get out of the way as soon as possible: "[Jesus] must increase, but I must decrease" (John 3:30). John's mission—which should be the mission of every preacher—was to prepare the people to look in one direction. In fact, you could say it was to do two things: to prepare and to direct. The preparation was to bring his hearers to the point of repentance—to "bear fruit worthy of repentance" (Matt. 3:8). The direction was to point to a person—when John saw Jesus coming toward him, he said, "Look, the Lamb of God, who takes away the sin of the world. This is He of whom I said, 'After me comes a Man who is preferred before me, for He was before me.'" (John 1:29–30).

The task of leadership in worship is to prepare a people and point to a person. The person is the pre-existent, eternal Son of God. We must all be brought to the point where we adore Jesus. The burden of my heart for my own church is that, as a consequence of the worship there (and I refer to the whole service), the members of the congregation will leave with a passionate love of Jesus and desire to adore Him. And to do this, I as a leader must diminish.

The second thing to remember about leadership in worship is that the leader should see and follow the Spirit. The only leadership that is able to lead people out in worship and love of Jesus is leadership that is itself under the guidance of the Holy

Spirit. Jesus said, "God is Spirit, and those who worship Him must worship Him in spirit and truth" (John 4:24).

John 1:32 is a very interesting verse: "Then John bore witness, saying, 'I saw the Spirit descending from heaven like a dove." The one who wants to lead worship by the Spirit must first discern the Spirit himself. Paul said to Timothy, "The farmer who labors should be first to partake of the crops" (2 Tim. 2:6).

The tragedy of today's generation is that most of its leaders are merely followers. They watch which way the people are going and then jump out in front and say, "Follow me." They are just like the politicians who hire Mr. Gallup to find out what the people are thinking. But for leadership in worship it is necessary to see the Spirit, and the only one who can see the Spirit is the person who is already filled with the Spirit.

One of the worst things that can happen to a church is to have a leader who is not a man of God, for then the worship will be a noise and a show.

"So," someone may say, "how can we know that our leader sees the Spirit?"

Well, the test is to see where he leads you. John 1:32 says, "I saw the Spirit descending from heaven like a dove, and it remained on Him." With what result? John released his followers to follow Jesus: "Again, the next day John was standing with two of his disciples. Looking upon Jesus as He walked, he said, 'Look, the Lamb of God!' The two disciples heard him speak, and they followed Jesus" (John 1:35–37).

The leader of a church is led by the Spirit when the members of his church fall in love with the Lord Jesus Christ.

Young believers need milk at first, but then they have to be weaned. Just as growing children and adults need meat, so Christians must learn to think for themselves. It is only a selfish parent who wants to hold onto a child forever. Leadership in worship must be a leadership that keeps out of the way as much as possible and enables the people to see and follow Jesus in the power of the Holy Spirit.

CHAPTER 14

LEARNING FROM ANGELS

And one cried to another and said, "Holy,
holy, holy, is the Lord of hosts."

—ISAIAH 6:3

THE MOST PERFECT worshippers of God in all His creation inside or outside the universe are the angels. Presumably when we, the redeemed, are glorified, we will be able to worship God perfectly too; because in heaven we will, as Robert Murray McCheyne put it: "Love [God] with unsinning [hearts]."[1] But in the meantime our worship is imperfect, so surely we can learn from angels.

Angels are created, non-material, spiritual beings who cannot be seen with the naked eye unless they choose to reveal themselves to us. There are various categories of angels: cherubim, seraphim, messengers (the Greek word, *angellos*, which we translate as "angel," means "messenger"), principalities, and powers. We know the names of two prominent angels, Michael and Gabriel, but it wouldn't surprise me to learn that every angel has his own name.

There are two orders of angels: fallen angels and unfallen angels. Jude 6 refers to those angels "who did not keep to their first domain, but forsook their own dwelling," and says that God has reserved them "in everlasting chains under darkness for the judgment of the great day." According to Peter in 2 Peter 2:4, they are cast down to hell. Here the word *hell* is the translation of the Greek word *tartarus*. But we don't, in fact, know what *tartarus* means. It is not used anywhere else in the Bible, and it is probably wrong to translate it as "hell." The word probably refers to the sphere of God's creation, which we have not yet seen, where fallen angels exist.

C. S. Lewis suggests that there is a hierarchy among the fallen angels. Satan is their commander-in-chief, and they are classed as evil spirits, devils, and demons.

The unfallen angels are those who did not give in to Satan's rebellion. It would seem that they are the elect angels, who Paul refers to in 1 Timothy 5:21, and who, according to the writer of the Hebrews are "all ministering spirits sent out to minister to those who will inherit salvation" (Heb. 1:14).

There is some hint in the Bible that the angels want to learn from us. 1 Peter 1:10, 12 says, "Concerning this salvation, the prophets who prophesied of the grace that should come to you have inquired and searched diligently.... It was revealed to them that they were not serving themselves but you, concerning the things which are now reported to you by those who have preached the gospel to you through the Holy Spirit, who was sent from heaven—*things into which the angels desire to look*" (emphasis added).

I confess that I have never understood this verse, though I have read a lot of speculation about it, perhaps not all of it unprofitable. We can say this: the angels know nothing of the joy of being redeemed.

Many years ago Johnson Oatman, Jr. wrote a great song, the refrain of which ran:

> Holy, holy, is what the angels sing,
> And I expect to help them make the courts of heaven
> ring;
> But when I sing redemption's story, they will fold their
> wings,
> For angels never felt the joys that our salvation brings.[2]

And according to Joseph Ton, our testimony in the world matters also because of on-looking angels. Our obedience in trial, suffering, or persecution is important because angels are witnessing our faithfulness.

On many occasions angels have sustained and protected God's people. Psalm 34:7 says, "The angel of the LORD camps around those who fear Him, and delivers them." And in Psalm 91:11 we read, "He shall give His angels charge over you to guard you in all your ways." Now exactly when God dispatches an angel, or angels, to come to our side, I do not know. Perhaps it is only in a time of trial. Or maybe at the time of our conversion an angel immediately comes alongside us and remains with us, which I believe to be the case.

Hebrews 1:14 says that angels are "ministering spirits sent out to minister to those who *will* inherit salvation." So it could be that an angel stands guard over God's elect from the moment of their birth. But whatever the case may be, always keep in mind that your angel has had tremendous experience in fighting the devil.

Although they know nothing of the joy of redemption, angels have resisted Satan's revolt and have therefore firsthand knowledge of how to resist the devil. For you can be sure that, when Satan conspired to rebel, he tried to enlist every angel in heaven. And he succeeded with some. But those who did not acquiesce know how to withstand him. So we should be able to learn from them by virtue of this fact alone.

We are dealing here with a delicate mystery because it is difficult to tell the difference between the function of angels and the work of the Holy Spirit. I can't see, humanly speaking, why there should be any need for angels. Surely the third person of the Trinity, who is the omnipotent, omniscient, omnipresent God, could accomplish anything angels are called upon to do. But God has chosen to employ angels.

The first thing we can learn about angels with reference to worship is that angels adore God alone. The prophet Isaiah was given to see with his spiritual eyes what is going on in heaven all the time. (And I cannot deny feeling envious of Isaiah!) He says, "In the year that King Uzziah died I saw the LORD sitting on a throne, high and lifted up, and His train filled the temple. Above it stood the seraphim. Each one had six wings. With two he covered his face, and with two he covered his feet, and with two he flew. One cried to another and said: 'Holy, holy, holy, is the LORD of Hosts; the whole earth is full of His glory'" (Isa. 6:1–3).

Everything is done out of love for God. Whatever feeling angels may have for us, their priority is the glory of God. The angel standing over you is on God's side. He is a messenger, and he is for you, but he adores God alone. And nothing will ever divert him from that loyalty.

The second thing is that angels refuse to be worshipped. When John was given his glorious revelation on the Isle of Patmos, he fell at the feet of the angel. And I have always been surprised at this. You would have thought that John, "the disciple whom Jesus loved, who also leaned against His bosom" (John 21:20), who had had a lifetime's experience of God, would have known better. But Revelation 19:10 says, "I fell at his feet to worship him. But he said to me, 'See that you not do that. I am your fellow servant, and of your brothers who hold the testimony of Jesus. Worship God! For the testimony of Jesus is the spirit of prophecy.'"

And if this were not enough, John went on to make the same mistake again. In Revelation 22:8 we read: "I, John, am he who saw and heard these things. When I heard and saw them, I fell down to worship at the feet of the angel who showed me these things." And he got the same reaction: "But he said to me, 'See that you not do that. For I am your fellow servant, and of your brothers the prophets, and of those who keep the words of this book. Worship God!'" (v. 9).

This teaches us not to be impatient with people who give in to idolatry or do things we don't approve of, and also that the greatest service we can perform is to direct men to God. The angel did not want any recognition or worship. He pointed to Christ—and in that he was like the Holy Spirit. We must always seek to encourage others to worship God. It never does any good to let people admire us too much as sooner or later we will disillusion them.

When Paul wrote to the church at Corinth, he had to acknowledge that there were arguments among them. For the people were saying, "'I am of Paul,' or 'I am of Apollos,' or 'I am of Cephas,' or 'I am of Christ.'" (1 Cor. 1:12). So Paul said to them, "Who then is Paul, and who is Apollos, but ministers by whom you believed, even as the Lord gave to each one? I have planted, Apollos watered, but God gave the increase. So then neither is he who plants nor he who waters anything, but God who gives the increase" (1 Cor. 3:5–7). We must release others to worship God. And we must not follow any Christian leader uncritically, for we will have to stand before God on our own someday.

Third, angels exist to do God's will. As we have seen, they are God's messengers to us, and they reveal God's will to us. This is why an angel sometimes has to do something that hurts us. When Zechariah, the father of John the Baptist, did not believe what the angel Gabriel told him, Gabriel said to him, "And now you will be silent and unable to speak until the day that these things happen, because you did not believe my words, which will be fulfilled in their season" (Luke 1:20). And at once Zechariah was unable to speak. You can't argue or bargain with an angel: they do what they are ordered to do.

In His story of the rich man and Lazarus, Jesus said that, when Lazarus died, he was "carried by the angels to Abraham's presence" (Luke 16:22). And it is also the awful truth that angels will escort the lost to their eternal doom. We can learn from this that we must never become so involved with people— even our closest friends—that we risk being influenced by them. We are to obey God alone.

Perfect worship of God consists of doing His will. The depth of our worship is not revealed by how high we raise our hands or how high we jump when we get excited. We worship perfectly when we obey God.

A fourth thing we may learn is that angels never tire of

worshipping God. Revelation 4:8, although not a reference to angels, shows us what kind of worship there is in heaven. This verse says of the four beasts, "All day and night, without ceasing, they were saying: 'Holy, holy, holy, Lord God Almighty.'" Throughout many thousands of years, ever since they were created, the angels have been worshipping God. And they have never tired of it or let their worship become commonplace. And we too will experience the highest joy throughout eternity in the sheer adoration and worship of God.

Fifth, we can see that angels worship the Lord Jesus Christ. The focal point of the worship of angels is the triune God. Now God is in three persons—*persona*, to use Tertullian's Latin word—God the Father, the Son, and the Holy Spirit. Jesus, the Son, the second person of the Trinity, is eternal, and I have no doubt that the angels worshipped him as the eternal Logos—the Word—before He was made flesh in Bethlehem. Hebrews 1:6 says, "And again, when He brings the firstborn into the world, He says: 'Let all the angels of God worship Him.'" The angels, therefore, worshipped Jesus when He came, as the God-man, into the world.

They worship Him though they do not know the joy of redemption. They know nothing of the shed blood of the Cross being applied to them. How much more ought we to worship the Lord Jesus Christ, we, who were lost, hell bound, and hell deserving, but who have been rescued because Jesus took upon Himself the punishment that we deserve and died on a cross? How much more should we fall on our faces and adore Him?

And another thing about angels is that they perceive the true essence of God's character: "One cried to another and said: 'Holy, holy, holy, is the LORD of hosts'" (Isa. 6:3). They know that God is holy. How do you define *holiness*? One theologian has described it as "the otherness of God." I think he meant that even if there were no such thing as sin, God would be still totally "other." God will never cease to be God throughout eternity; He will never cease to be independent of both created and redeemed beings.

So the seraphim, who don't even know what sin is, actually cover their faces with their wings in the presence of God. Isaiah says of them: "Each one had six wings. With two he covered his face, and with two he covered his feet, and with two he flew" (Isa. 6:2). And they praise God for His essential nature. What would the sight of a holy God do to us, who are sinners? It could only have the effect of making us say, with Isaiah, "Woe is me! For I am undone because I am a man of unclean lips, and I dwell in the midst of a people of unclean lips. For my eyes have seen the King, the LORD of Hosts" (Isa. 6:5).

Moreover, even though they have been in His presence and have been worshipping Him for millions of years, the angels still show great reverence for God. Humanly speaking, once we get to know a person whom we have previously only seen from afar, we lose a bit of the awe we had of them. But with God, the closer you get to Him, and the better you know Him, the more reverence you feel for Him.

We see from Isaiah 6:3 that the angels talk to one another about God: "One cried to another and said: 'Holy, holy, holy, is the LORD of Hosts.'" And their conversation reveals great wonder and reverence. Never let us be flippant or familiar when we talk of God or to God. If we are superficial or offhand, we reveal merely how far we are from God and true worship.

I wish with all my heart that Christians would talk to one another about God. We talk about the weather, about sports, about our work, about television programs, and about other people and what is happening to them, yet how strangely silent we are about God, even after the church services! Surely this is one of the greatest of all indications that our lives are empty of God, and we know nothing of true worship. "For out of the abundance of the heart the mouth speaks," said Jesus (Matt. 12:34). And if our mouths are silent about God in our day-to-day conversation, what does that say about our hearts?

The next thing we can learn from angels is that they also perceive the extent of God's glory in the universe. Isaiah 6:3 says, "...the whole earth is full of His glory." The angels see

God's glory everywhere. And the reason is that angels can see the physical and the spiritual simultaneously. We are limited to what is tangible and material. But angels can see everything.

Remember what Elisha said in 2 Kings 6? He looked around and saw armies on every side, and his servant was scared to death. It didn't seem as if they had a chance. "And [Elisha] said, 'Do not be afraid, for there are more with us than with them.' Then Elisha prayed, 'Lord, open his eyes and let him see.' So the Lord opened the eyes of the young man, and he saw that the mountain was full of horses and chariots of fire surrounding Elisha" (vv. 16–17).

The angels can see what is there, and if we could too, we would face a thousand worlds. Our worship should leave us with tremendous confidence, for in the battles we fight, "there are more with us than with them." Our enemy is God's enemy. And God's glory is not just in heaven but in all the earth.

And as we have already seen, angels know how to resist the devil. They have great experience in resisting him, and they do it properly. In Jude 9 we read, "Yet Michael the archangel, when contending with the devil in a dispute about the body of Moses, did not dare to pronounce upon him a railing judgment. But he said, 'The Lord rebuke you!'"

The archangel Michael did not take Satan on himself. He showed contempt for him and said, "The Lord rebuke you!" Don't let us ever be stupid enough to think we can take the devil on alone. Like the angels, we must say, "The Lord rebuke you!" If they can do it, how much more should we be able to, who have the blood of Jesus as our covering?

And finally, we learn that the angels rejoice in the conversion of the lost. Jesus says, "Likewise, I tell you, there is joy in the presence of the angels of God over one sinner who repents" (Luke 15:10). And so we too should rejoice. We should not be like the brother of the prodigal son, who felt that he had not been treated well. Instead, we ought to say with his father, "But it was fitting to be merry and be glad, for this brother of yours was dead and is alive again; he was lost and is found" (Luke 15:32).

That is the right way to look at anybody who has come to Christ. And the fact that the angels rejoice shows what they must think of evangelism and our going out to save the lost: they are with us.

We can learn from angels. And the more we learn, the better we will worship God and the more they will rejoice. Have you ever thought that when we meet with other Christians to worship God, our angels meet together too? The more we worship, the more they rejoice. If we could only see the expression on their faces, we would know if we were getting our worship right. For that is what we are after—to become true worshippers so that the glory of God may be acknowledged on earth as in heaven.

CHAPTER 15

SPIRITUAL WARFARE IN WORSHIP

For our fight is not against flesh and blood, but against principalities, against powers... against spiritual forces of evil in the heavenly places.

—EPHESIANS 6:12

IN CHAPTER 14 we saw that there are two types of angels—fallen and unfallen. I want now to focus on fallen angels—fallen angels who are very much alive as we see from Paul's words to the Ephesians above. Rarely have I experienced such opposition and conflict as when I was preparing the material for this chapter—which is a fairly strong hint that Satan doesn't like any effort on our part to unmask him. It also shows how threatened Satan is by worship. The devil is described in a number of ways in Scripture, for example, "the god of this world" (2 Cor. 4:4); "the prince of the power of the air" (Eph. 2:2); "a roaring lion" (1 Pet. 5:8); and "the accuser of our brothers" (Rev. 12:10).

The problem of evil is unsolvable this side of heaven. We just don't know why God allowed evil to come into the world. And the Scriptures are not as clear as we would perhaps like them to be on the subject of the origin of Satan. Theologians have pieced some of the scriptures together and drawn from them a few conclusions, which, as far as I know, cannot be disproved. What we believe to be true is that Satan was known as Lucifer, and that he fell, taking a number of angels with him. Isaiah 14:12 says, "How are you fallen from heaven, O Lucifer, son of the morning!" Jude refers to "the angels who did not keep to their first domain (v. 6), and 2 Peter 2:4 says, "God did not spare the angels that sinned, but cast them down to hell..."

Some have speculated, from Revelation 12:4—"His tail drew a third of the stars of heaven, and threw them to the earth"— that Satan took a third of the angels with him. And Augustine speculated that the number of God's elect will be the same as the number of angels who sinned.[1]

Exactly what happened when evil emerged, and why God allowed it, we just don't know, and trying to figure it all out is unprofitable speculation. If we understood everything, then there would be no need for faith.

What is not speculation is this: our greatest enemy is Satan, who is also the greatest enemy of Christ. What is also not speculation is that Satan's doom is already mapped out. It is described in Revelation 20:10: "The devil, who deceived them, was cast into the lake of fire and brimstone where the beast and the false prophet were. They will be tormented day and night forever and ever."

Satan already knows that this is his doom, and he is also aware that his time is limited. Revelation 12:12 says, "Woe unto the inhabitants of the earth and the sea! For the devil has come down to you in great wrath, because he knows that his time is short." And this is one reason why he is so angry.

Something else that is certain about Satan is that he will try to take everybody down with him. I read in the paper about a man who, when he discovered that he had AIDS, tried to spread it to as many people as he could. "If I'm going to die," he said, "I want others to die too." And that's like Satan. He wants to take everybody with him.

He tries to do this by keeping people from being saved. He is called "the god of this world" who blinds "the minds of those who do not believe, lest the light of the glorious gospel of Christ, who is the image of God, should shine on them" (2 Cor. 4:4). Whenever anybody is not saved, it shows that Satan has succeeded with them.

When Satan fails and people are converted, he then does all that he can to keep them from holiness. He will try to get them to grieve and quench the Spirit because he wants to keep them from a state of blissful worship.

New Christians need to be taught these things. They also need to know that the devil will attempt to push us to extreme views about him. He will either try to get us to be over-preoccupied with him or to disregard him completely. If we become preoccupied with the occult, with witchcraft, even if it is on the grounds that we just want to learn more about the dangers of Satan, we open ourselves up to oppression, if not possession, by evil spirits. So we need to be very careful. At the other extreme, if Satan can get us to discount as rubbish anything to do with the occult, he will be very pleased because then we will fail to be on our guard.

Here are nine more things about the devil: he is jealous, insecure, vengeful, and persistent. He is also unteachable (he never learns from his mistakes), a liar and a deceiver, and he is full of hate. But, most of all, he is resistible.

As I grew up, my father used to say to me, "Son, remember that the devil is crafty. He is second only to God in power and wisdom." And that is absolutely true. The devil is second only to God, but he is *second*, and that is why he is resistible. As Peter put it: "Resist him firmly in the faith" (1 Pet. 5:9).

"Resist the devil, and he will flee from you," said James (James 4:7). That is a promise, and it works!

Because of his jealousy Satan cannot tolerate Jesus being exalted. A film star may hate hearing a rival being praised or getting good reviews. Similarly, Satan hates Jesus being exalted; he cannot bear to hear the truth preached or to see a united church where the Spirit is ungrieved and unbound.

Thus all our efforts to get our worship right will make him angry. We need to be aware of how he works and know how to combat him. His strategy is to devour, deceive, and demoralize. Peter wrote: "Be sober and watchful, because your adversary the devil walks around as a roaring lion, seeking whom he may devour" (1 Pet. 5:8). He devours the work of God, and if he can, he will abort it before it has a chance to work. He is therefore always in at the beginning: "The dragon stood before the woman who was ready to give birth, to devour her Child as soon as He was born" (Rev. 12:4). Satan doesn't wait around for something to get started to see if it is going to be a threat to him. He already knows whether it will be or not, and he's in there right at the beginning.

I've already written in chapter 7 about the importance of expectancy before worship. As we come to worship, we should be undisturbed in our heart and spirit—for our preparation for worship will often be the object of Satan's attacks. Because he does not like the idea of a lot of people, all of whom enjoy the ungrieved Spirit, coming together, he will do anything that he can to disturb us just before the service. Have you ever noticed how Satan will attack you on a Sunday morning? Someone oversleeps and isn't ready. The toast is burnt, and the coffee spilled. Or just as you are going out of the door, you can't find the keys! And if you finally make it to church, you find that somebody is there you didn't want to see. Or perhaps someone doesn't speak to you or doesn't smile at you as you are coming in at the door, and the whole service is ruined for you while you wonder what you can have done to them.

This is the devil. The first time we started singing choruses in Westminster Chapel, about a dozen uninvited people came out and danced, including a sexy young lady in a miniskirt. This produced a shocked reaction. What the devil was trying to do, I believe, was to frighten us off, but I knew we had to persist, both in our new emphasis on evangelism and in livelier worship. That's the way the devil works, wasting no time in trying to destroy the work of the Spirit. Jonathan Edwards used to say, "Remember when the Church is revived, the devil is also revived."

Satan goes for new converts, trying to stop any kind of follow-up; and he attacks people who make a fresh commitment by trying to stop them acting on what they have been shown.

For example, when people pray about tithing, the devil is likely to bring to their minds every excuse for not tithing. Similarly, he will try to discourage those who are considering getting involved in evangelism—putting thoughts in their minds such as: "It's not my personality," "It's too cold," or "Maybe later..."

Satan will try to devour the whole of our worship too. One way is by trying to push us into extreme positions; for example, he persuades us to opt for stilted singing or for complete chaos; for deathlike silence or empty noise; for teaching at the expense of singing or vice versa.

Sometimes he tries to destroy our worship simply by trying to make us lose our concentration. He will try to draw our attention to everything under the sun in order to get our minds to wander. Often, when we have decided to spend time in prayer, we begin to think of things we must do, and before we know it, the time has gone, and we need to do something else. Second, Satan is out to deceive. Revelation 12:9 describes him as "that ancient serpent called the Devil and Satan, who deceives the whole world."

How does he set about his deception? In 2 Corinthians 11:14, Satan is called "an angel of light," which means that he uses apparently respectable means and people to deceive us. He tries first to lure us away from "the simplicity that is in Christ." As 2 Corinthians 11:3 says, "But I fear that somehow, as the serpent deceived Eve through his trickery, so your minds might be led astray from the simplicity that is in Christ."

Simplicity in worship may be one of his targets. He may get people involved in intellectual, formal types of worship that are a long way from the spirit of true worship.

Or he tries to lure us away from the truth and towards the counterfeit. Paul says: "For if he who comes preaches another Jesus, whom we have not preached, or if you receive another spirit, which you have not received, or another gospel, which you have not accepted, you might submit to it readily enough" (2 Cor. 11:4). The devil doesn't want the glorification of our sovereign Redeemer or the manifestation of the Holy Spirit, so he will perhaps lead us to settle for something which is staid, merely sentimental, or sheer entertainment.

Satan will divert us from any strong emphasis on the gospel or on sovereign grace, from the blood of Jesus or the majesty of God. He will also try to lead us away from any working of the unbound Spirit in the church. All his intelligence and powers of deception will be directed either towards a dilution of the gospel or a quenching of the Spirit.

Third, Satan is out to demoralize: "Now the salvation and the power and the kingdom of our God and the authority of His Christ have come, for the accuser of our brothers, who accused them before our God day and night, has been cast down" (Rev. 12:10).

How does Satan accuse? Sometimes he tells us that we are not saved. Or if he can't succeed with that, he tries to convince us that God has finished with us and that we are irreparably out of His will. Nothing is more demoralizing to a Christian than this. But let me give you a rule of thumb here: all oppression is of the devil. Dr. Martyn Lloyd-Jones used to say to me, "God never oppresses us."

Another method of accusing and demoralizing us is to tell us that we are not fit to worship God as we are. The devil reminds us of some weakness or failing in our life—as a Christian or a student or a parent—and he says, "You must get that right before you can worship God. You let others do the worshipping today. You're not in a fit state to do anything." He tries to get in during the week, and if he fails there, he tries on Sunday morning. If we lose our temper or give in to some other weakness, he says to us: "You're not fit." But God never says that.

A third way Satan tries to demoralize us is by creating disturbances in worship. It may be a baby crying, a drunk shouting out, or any untimely disturbances that get us to say, "Oh, what's the use?" It is by demoralizing the saints that Satan succeeds in getting revival to tarry.

When Satan succeeds, he can say, "I'm not going to have any problems there today!" And we will not even realize that the

Spirit has gone. Remember that Samson "did not know that the LORD had left him" (Judges 16:20). We will only find out later, when we try to do something and realize we are doing it in our own strength. Remember, though, that we cannot lose our salvation, for Paul says, "And do not grieve the Holy Spirit of God, in whom you are sealed for the day of redemption" (Eph. 4:30).

So what are we to do in the face of Satan's strategies? The answer is that we must refuse to give place to him. We must realize that Satan's strategy is aimed to produce one thing—a grieved Holy Spirit. That is all he wants. And if he achieves that, then he has won.

But look at Revelation 12:11: "They overcame him by the blood of the Lamb and by the word of their testimony, and they loved not their lives unto the death."

The blood of Jesus tells me that I can always worship God. Yes, I am unworthy. Yes, I have sinned. Yes, I am not all that I ought to be. But that is why Jesus died. In the words of John Newton:

> Be Thou my shield and hiding place,
> That, sheltered near Thy side,
> I may my fierce accuser face,
> And tell him Thou hast died.[2]

The blood of Jesus is a free invitation to worship God now. Whoever we are and whatever our state, we can always resort to the blood, and that brings us up to the level of the most worthy "saint."

> Just as I am, without one plea,
> But that thy blood was shed for me,
> And that thou bidd'st me come to thee,
> O Lamb of God, I come, I come.[3]

God wants us to believe this, but Satan wants us to doubt it because, when we are convinced that the blood of Jesus was shed for us, we are on our way, and Satan falls.

The saints must affirm unashamedly that God has accepted them. They overcome the devil not only through the blood of Jesus, but by "the word of their testimony" (Rev. 12:11). It is one thing to have the blood of Jesus offered to us; it is another to act upon it, confident that nothing can stop us. When we affirm by the word of our testimony all that the blood of Jesus was meant to do, then Satan vanishes as quickly as darkness dispelled by light.

It is by the word of our testimony that we prove we are indeed resisting the devil. In terms of worship, we are to enter into the praying and the preaching and the singing with all our hearts, and shut everything else out. We are to let ourselves get caught up in the joy of all that is happening.

The final aspect of the saint's strategy is selfless concern: "they loved not their lives unto the death" (Rev. 12:11). When we are caught up into spiritual worship, self-concern diminishes to nothing. Self-love is swallowed up by a love for God's glory.

Something else that will also vanish is self-consciousness— what others may think of us. There is a warning here: Satan will conquer us to the extent that we allow self-concern to pre-occupy our thoughts. But there is also a promise: the extent to which we become enamored with the grace and mercy and blood of Christ is the extent to which we will find ourselves living in the realm out of which martyrs are born.

Joseph Ton said, "The most dangerous person in the world is the man who is not afraid to die."

"They loved not their lives unto the death." May our worship leave us in a state of selfless love for Jesus. Then we will be able to face any obstacle: the office, the friend who betrayed us, our besetting sin, that overwhelming worry, that dreadful fear, and every attack of Satan. Why? Because God accepts us, and that is what matters: "If God is for us, who can be against us?" (Rom. 8:31).

CHAPTER 16

...WITH GIVING

Bring all the tithes into the storehouse...and test Me now in this, says the Lord of Hosts, if I will not open for you the windows of heaven and pour out for you a blessing, that there will not be room enough to receive it.

—MALACHI 3:10 .

I BELIEVE THAT NOT only is giving a part of worship but that it may also constitute a much greater part than many of us have thought. I say this for three reasons. I can give the first by reminding you of the definition of *worship* which I gave in Chapter 1: worship is "the response to, and/or preparation for, the preached Word." How we respond to the preached Word will show how much we truly worship. And how we respond to, and prepare for, God's call to give according to the undoubted biblical pattern will largely reflect the quality of our worship.

The second reason I have for saying that giving is an integral part of worship is that worship must be a matter of the heart. And I am absolutely convinced that having a stingy heart—a mean spirit—inhibits our worship. Imagine that you have put a strong rubber band around your fingers and now you are trying to open them. You just won't be able to until the band is cut or released in some way. Well, I believe that many people are in bondage, and would like to break out, but haven't succeeded because they have not made the commitment to tithe.

My third reason is that in the Old Testament tithing consistently reflected the response of gratitude which the patriarchs felt towards God. And these towering figures—Abraham,

114

Isaac, Jacob—were raised up by God four hundred years before the Law came. This is a vital point. It is not true that to decide to tithe is to go back to a life lived under law: it is to return to the example set by Abraham. And the heart of Paul's teaching is that we take our cue on how we become Christians and how we live the Christian life from Abraham.

Jesus said, "Your father Abraham rejoiced to see My day. He saw it and was glad" (John 8:56). And Paul said, "Therefore know that those who are of faith are the sons of Abraham" (Gal. 3:7). The Law came in later, but it could not ignore the promise God made to Abraham.

Abraham's story is thrilling. His nephew, Lot, had been caught and captured in the crossfire of a war that was going on between several kings. God enabled Abraham not only to rescue Lot, but also to retrieve Lot's possessions and gain much other spoil as well. At which point Melchizedek, king of Salem, who is called in Genesis 14:18 "the priest of God Most High," came to Abraham and blessed him. And Genesis 14:20 says, "[Abraham] gave him a tenth of everything." Now one might think that Abraham could have given all the spoils to Melchizedek because, after all, Abraham had not been expecting to gain anything when he rescued Lot. But he gave one tenth. Why the tithe? The answer is that the tithe is the consistent pattern of the Spirit for all times. When God made the decision in eternity to send his Son into the world, He knew that the gospel would have to be supported. Tithing was not an afterthought in God's scheme of things.

Abraham was not the only one who gave the tithe. Jacob crowned one of the peak moments of his life with the words, "and from all that You give me I will surely give a tenth to You" (Gen. 28:22). It is a beautiful story. God had come to Jacob at a time when he felt very unworthy, having stolen the birthright from his brother, Esau, and run away from home. At night he fell asleep on the bare ground, with stones for his pillow, and he had a dream—the famous vision of Jacob's ladder. In Jacob's dream God said to him, "Your descendants will be like the dust of the earth, and you will spread abroad to the west and to the east and to the north and to the south, and in you and in your descendants all the families of the earth will be blessed" (Gen. 28:14).

Jacob was so overcome that God should talk to him like this that "he called the name of that place Bethel" (v. 19). "Jacob vowed a vow, saying, 'If God will be with me and will protect me in this way that I go… then the LORD will be my God… and from all that You give me I will surely give a tenth to You'" (vv. 20–22).

Tithing has thus always been a part of true worship, that is, worship that is of the heart and precipitated by the Spirit of God. Both Abraham and Jacob were so overwhelmed by God's goodness that they gave back a tithe.

Thus we can see that the Law of Moses merely legalized tithing. What was the spontaneous and disciplined impulse of the patriarchs was made mandatory by the Law. Hence we read in Leviticus 27:30, "Any tithe of the land, whether seed of the land or fruit of the trees, belongs to the LORD. It is holy to the LORD." The tithe was the Lord's by right, and those who refused to tithe were therefore punished, for, as Malachi says, "Will a man rob God?" (Mal. 3:8). According to Malachi, ten percent is the Lord's already, whether it is given or not. The gospel era did not introduce any new standard of righteousness. The righteousness that God requires has always been the same. But now God does not, as it were, put a pistol to our heads; instead He puts us on our honor and asks us to give from our hearts. And have we not much more reason to give gladly and gratefully than people who lived in Moses's day since we have known the love and grace of Jesus?

Just as sin was present in the world before the Ten Commandments were set out, so tithing was God's way before the Law came in. Just as love fulfills the Law by keeping the commandments, so, I believe, a Spirit-filled, grateful man or woman who truly wants to worship God will always be convicted to tithe. One of the reasons why people are so quick to argue against tithing is just because they are convicted and are repressing what they know to be true. They have developed what a psychologist would call a "reaction formation" and exhibit a great need to prove that they do not have to tithe. In the words of Shakespeare, they "protest too much."[1]

It is instructive to consider Jesus's attitude to tithing. Jesus said, "Woe to you, scribes and Pharisees, hypocrites! You tithe mint and dill and cumin, but have neglected the weightier matters of the law: justice and mercy and faith. These you ought to have done without leaving the others undone" (Matt. 23:23).

Jesus is here exposing the self-righteousness of the Pharisees. Yet he ends his condemnation of them with the words, "without leaving the others [tithing] undone." Jesus approved of tithing.

Many people will only do things when they "feel led." They are unwilling simply to accept what the Bible says but want a special word. I have already spoken about Psalm 50:12 in connection with prayer, but it applies equally here. God says, "If I were hungry, I would not tell you." In other words, we cannot guarantee that we will be so close to God that we will always catch these "special words." God wants us to obey His Word in the Bible. On the subject of tithing, God has already spoken. Why should some people think they are so spiritual that God is going to give them special attention or tell them something different?

Some people say they disagree with tithing because it is too little—or at least the barest minimum that ought to be given. But I have discovered something about those who say this. If such people are asked to check their records, they find that, almost invariably, they do not even come up to the tenth in their giving! God wants us to show what we think of His way by having discipline, as Abraham or Jacob had discipline. Every Christian, by definition, ought to accept tithing as a commitment. To say you are a Christian means that you have taken on the name of Christ, who told us to tithe. And a Christian is a child of Abraham, who set the example. Christians owe it to God to live on ninety percent of their income. For every hundred dollars that we earn, ten dollars belong to God. If we make thirty thousand dollars a year, we will have to put three thousand dollars into the storehouse.

I know that most Christians don't tithe because they have never been taught it, which is why I am taking such care to explain the principles.

I would like to give you some advice—and I know what I am talking about. I was a Jonah on this subject, and ran away, until God swallowed me up. Just after my wife and I were married, we were under great financial pressure. I came home one day feeling very discouraged and longing for a word from God. But God seemed to be hiding His face from me. The only verse I could get was Malachi 3:8: "Will a man rob God?" I got this verse three days in a row, and I said, "Lord, I want encouragement. I don't want that."

I wasn't tithing then. We were so deeply in debt that I just kept saying, "Lord, you know I have to pay my bills. You know the most religious thing I can do is to pay my bills." That was the way I justified not tithing.

But things didn't get any better. Two years later we were deeper in debt. At last, one day I decided to give God His tenth. We didn't get out of debt in a month or even a year. It took two years. But it happened, and now I wouldn't not tithe for anything in the world. And I have lived that way for twenty-five years.

The practical advice I want to give out of my experience is this: take the tithe off the top before any other bill is paid. Consider that ten percent "hot money" and give it to God as quickly as you can. Let it lie around and you will spend it every time. You will say, "Well, God understands we have to pay the milk bill, and the money's right there." There will always be something to use the money up.

A lot of people tithe fairly regularly, and think that's enough. But how would your husband or wife feel if you were faithful for fifty-one weeks of the year but were unfaithful for the other week? So how do you think God feels when we hold back and justify what we keep for ourselves by saying, "God knows I have to pay my bills"?

Paul taught the Corinthians to be disciplined and regular in their tithing. He said, "On the first day of the week let every one of you lay in store, as God has prospered him" (1 Cor. 16:2). Note that we are not all asked to give the same amount. Tithing is very fair. The wealthy man must pay as much for a loaf of bread or a pound of minced beef as the poor man. But when it comes to your income, God says, "You keep ninety percent—I'll take ten percent."

The wealthy man will be taxed by the IRS at a rate of over thirty percent. But God only wants ten percent.

In 2 Corinthians 9 Paul shows, first, that he has taught these people the importance of giving, and second, that they had, as a result of this, become a great example to others. Verse 2 says, "I know your willingness." The Phillips translation is, "I know how willing you are." The NIV puts it, "I know your eagerness to help." Paul had not seen the Corinthians for a while, and he felt led of the Spirit to remind them of certain principles. So in effect he says, "I have been bragging about you, and now that I'm coming to you again, I know you won't forget that or what I am going to tell you." This indicates that we not only need to be taught the principles of giving, but that we all need to be reminded of them.

What are the principles which Paul lays down here?

The first is that giving will do as much for us as it does for those who receive the money. As J. B. Phillips puts it: "Giving does not only help the one who receives."[2] Paul says, "He who sows sparingly will also reap sparingly, and he who sows bountifully will also reap bountifully" (2 Cor. 9:6). And have you not found this to be true?

Paul tells us here that God is a rewarder. Many people maintain that they do not want any reward. All right—that's fine. But most of us are weak enough and human enough to need a little motivation. And God will give it to us. He wants us to know that He blesses those who tithe. His Word says, "Honor the LORD with your substance, and with the first fruits of all your increase; so your barns will be filled with plenty, and your presses will burst out with new wine" (Prov. 3:9–10). Dr. O. S. Hawkins comments, "When the Church releases their tithe to God and become hilarious givers, that's when the windows of blessing in spiritual measure will be poured out."

"Bring all the tithes into the storehouse," said Malachi, "that there may be food in My house" (Mal. 3:10). In Malachi's day, *storehouse* meant the temple, and today it means our own local church. God loves the church—it is the apple of His eye—and the tithe should go to the church. If you can give more than the tenth, then you are free to distribute it elsewhere, to Christian work at home and overseas, but the tithe must go to the storehouse of the church.

Paul's second principle is that giving, in order to be a part of the worship, must come from the heart. "Let every man give according to the purposes in his heart" (2 Cor. 9:7). This is because we are not under the Law of Moses, but of Christ. God puts us on our honor, and at the end of the day we have to decide whether we believe that this is God's way for us or not. And God wants us to be generous and glad in our giving: "for God loves a cheerful giver" (2 Cor. 9:7).

I come now to the last of Paul's principles: God wants not only our tithe, but also our trust. This is how Paul puts it in 2 Corinthians 9:8: "God is able to make all grace abound toward you, so that you, always having enough of everything, may abound to every good work." Just three verse later 2 Corinthians 9:11 says, "So you will be enriched in everything to all bountifulness."

When we worship God and trust Him, when we give Him money that we could have kept for ourselves and used well, over the months and the years we will watch a mathematical impossibility take place. We will see the ninety percent of our money go as far as a hundred percent would have gone, and sometimes even further. I don't understand it, but this is what happens.

So make a commitment today that you are going to live like

this for the rest of your life. You will then find that you are not burdened and tied up by worries and fears about money. Frequently someone will come up to me and say, "Thank you for teaching me how to tithe." These people have discovered for themselves that when we trust and obey God, then He sets our spirits free because He loves to give back to us. And when our spirits are free, then we can worship Him from an overflowing and grateful heart.

CHAPTER 17

...WITH FASTING

*"But you, when you fast, anoint your head and wash
your face, so that you will not appear to men to be
fasting, but to your Father who is in secret...*

—MATTHEW 6:17–18

L IKE TITHING, MANY of us may not find the subject of
fasting pleasant because it comes down to the disciplined
impulse of the Spirit, but its rewards may well exceed our
greatest expectations. In fact, the more I have thought about
this subject, the more I have realized that if enough people in
a church took fasting seriously, its impact on the worship could
be quite dramatic.

Fasting is going without food to achieve a particular end. It
is a means to an end. There are non-religious reasons for fasting:
we may fast for health reasons, for example, or people may fast
as a protest to get the attention of the authorities and of world
opinion. But I do not want to deal with that kind of public
demonstration, and neither do I necessarily recommend it.

The Bible gives numerous accounts of fasting for spiritual reasons. It is often a sign of grief and mourning—even of despera-
tion. We read in Esther chapter 4: "When Mordecai learned
all that had been done, he tore his clothes and put on sackcloth with ashes, and went out into the midst of the city, and
cried with a loud and bitter cry. He went as far as the king's
gate because no one was allowed to enter into the king's gate
clothed with sackcloth. In each and every province where the
king's command and his decree came there was great mourning

among the Jews, and fasting, and weeping, and wailing. Many lay in sackcloth and ashes" (vv. 1–3).

Fasting is not something one does flippantly, with joy or gladness. Yet the New Testament assumption is that the disciples of Jesus should, and in fact do, fast. Jesus said, "Moreover, when you fast, do not be like the hypocrites with a sad countenance" (Matt. 6:16). Mark 2:19–20 says: "Jesus said to them, 'Can the wedding guests fast while the bridegroom is with them? As long as they have the bridegroom with them, they cannot fast. But the days will come when the bridegroom will be taken away from them, and then they will fast in those days.'"

The question of all of us is therefore: Is fasting something we should do in our twentieth-century churches, and if so, when should we fast?

According to the Bible, the people who fast fall into three categories. First, a nation. We read in Isaiah 58:2–3: "Yet they seek Me daily and delight to know My ways, as a nation that has done righteousness and has not forsaken the ordinance of their God... 'Why have we fasted...'" And in the Book of Nehemiah we see that the people of Israel felt the need to fast: "Now on the twenty-fourth day of this month the children of Israel were assembled with fasting and sackcloth, and there was dirt on them" (9:1).

So it is possible for a whole nation to fast. In the United Kingdom it is an unusual occurrence, but it has happened, although I am sorry to say that it was over sixty years ago. The last time the United Kingdom had a day of prayer and fasting was in the middle of World War II.

But the church may also fast. We read in Acts 13:2–3 that, "As [the church] worshipped the Lord and fasted, the Holy Spirit said, 'Set apart for Me Barnabas and Saul for the work to which I have called them.' Then after fasting and praying, they laid their hands on them and sent them off." And the "they" to whom Jesus refers in Mark 2:20 is also the church, the Bride of Christ: "But the days will come when the bridegroom will be taken away from them, and then they will fast in those days."

Lastly, an individual may fast. Moses fasted for forty days. Jesus fasted for forty days. And it was not unusual for David to fast. In Psalm 35:13 he says, "But as for me, when they were sick, my clothing was sackcloth; I humbled my soul with fasting." Read also Psalm 109:24: "My knees are weak through fasting."

The apostle Paul speaks of himself and his fellow workers in these words: "But in all things approving ourselves as the ministers of God, in much patience, in afflictions, in necessities, in distresses, in stripes, in imprisonments, in tumults, in labours, in watchings, in fastings" (2 Cor. 6:4–5, KJV). And again in 2 Corinthians 11:27 he says, "In weariness and painfulness, in sleeplessness often, in hunger and thirst, in fastings often..."

When we read that people like Moses, David, Paul, or our Lord Jesus Christ were given to fasting, we may see an answer to the question of why there is such a dearth of spiritual greatness at the present time. And if fasting is something new to us, we must ask ourselves whether God is leading us to engage in this particular spiritual enterprise.

This brings me to a consideration of the times when we should fast, for you might be thinking, "I'm willing to fast, but when do I do it?" I would therefore like to suggest five occasions on which fasting is justifiable.

I think the first of these would be when the burden we are under is so great that we do not really have a desire for food—for this may be a hint from God that we should fast. David experienced a time of great mourning when God smote the son born to him as a result of his adultery with Bathsheba. In 2 Samuel 12:15–16 we read, "The LORD struck the child that the wife of Uriah had born for David, and he became sick. David entreated God on behalf of the child. He fasted for a period, and he would go in and lie throughout the night on the ground."

The second occasion which justifies fasting is when we are about to embark on a very great task for God or have to make an important decision. At the beginning of His ministry, after His baptism, Jesus fasted. We read in Matthew 4:2: "And He had fasted for forty days and forty nights, and then He was hungry." And we have just seen how the church fasted and prayed before they sent Barnabas and Saul away to their work. Moreover, we are told of these two themselves, "When they had appointed elders for them in every church, with prayer and fasting, they commended them to the Lord in whom they believed" (Acts 14:23).

Perhaps you are conscious, as you read this, of something unusual ahead for which you need God's help. It may be, therefore, that in anticipation of what lies ahead, you should fast. Maybe you need to know God's will and don't know what to do. It is justifiable to fast because you need wisdom for something out there in the future.

A third reason is if we feel that God is hiding His face. When God does this, it may be a form of chastening: "for whom the Lord loves He disciplines, and scourges every son whom He receives" (Heb. 12:6). Perhaps we are in a rut or have known better days spiritually. Perhaps God is not as real as we have known Him to be, and we are not sure whether we have grieved Him or whether He has just chosen to hide His face for reasons we can't understand. When this happens, is it important to us? Is it something we really care about? If so, maybe we ought to fast. Perhaps God is hiding His face from us in order to drive us to our knees to seek Him. Joel wrote: "Yet even now, declares the LORD, return to Me with all your heart, and with fasting and with weeping and with mourning. Rend your heart, and not your garments; return to the LORD your God, for He is gracious and merciful, slow to anger, and abounding in steadfast love; and He relents from punishing. Who knows? He might turn aside and relent, and He might leave behind a blessing" (Joel 2:12–14).

The fourth occasion is when we have experienced delay in the answers to our prayers. In the Old Testament in particular we have accounts of situations where God did not step in as it had been hoped He would, and as a result the people fasted. In Ezra 8:22 the writer says, "For I was ashamed to ask the king for an escort of foot and horse soldiers to help us against the enemy on the way, because we had spoken to the king, saying, 'The hand of our God is upon all who seek Him for good, but His power and His wrath are against all who forsake Him.'" So he didn't go to the king. Instead, verse 23 says, "So we fasted and sought our God for this, and He was moved by our prayers."

Daniel, in the time of the captivity, realized one day that according to Jeremiah the prophet the captivity was only to last seventy years, and we read in chapter 9:3: "I set my face toward the Lord God to seek by prayer and supplications with fasting and sackcloth and ashes." So there is good reason to fast when there is a delay in answer to prayer or if you are not sure that God is going to step in.

How much do we really care that God should speak to us and answer our prayers? Missing a meal isn't a great discipline for some. But if you enjoy eating—and most of us do—then fasting is a good test of how important something is to us.

The fifth occasion that justifies fasting is when we feel the need of unusual power that we don't have. I base this assertion on the account in Matthew 17 of a case of demon possession, a case which was too big for the disciples to handle. When they asked, "Why could not we cast him out?" (v. 19), Jesus first said, "Because of your unbelief. For truly I say to you, if you have faith as a grain of mustard seed, you will say to this mountain, 'Move from here to there,' and it will move. And nothing will be impossible for you" (v. 20).

But He also gave them another reason: "But this kind does not go out except by prayer and fasting" (v. 21). Fasting should not, of course, be viewed as a way of twisting God's arm. We are not putting emotional pressure on God. We can't say, "Now I've fasted, You can see I'm serious, so please do Your bit." Fasting is a way of ensuring that we are completely dependent upon God and open to Him. It seeks spiritual emptiness and cleansing, and enables us to hear God speaking. In order to achieve this, our approach to fasting is very important.

First, fasting must be secret. Jesus said in Matthew 6:16–18:

"Moreover, when you fast, do not be like the hypocrites with a sad countenance. For they disfigure their faces so they may appear to men to be fasting. Truly I say to you, they have their reward. But you, when you fast, anoint your head and wash your face, so that you will not appear to men to be fasting, but to your Father who is in secret. And your Father who sees in secret will reward you openly."

There will always be a temptation to share with others the fact that we are fasting. In the time of the Pharisees, it was a sign of piety, and they would come out in public looking sad and mournful to let everybody see that they were fasting.

When I was a teenager, about fourteen or fifteen years old, God gave me a heart after His. When I came across this verse in Matthew and read the words, "Anoint your head," I wanted to get it right. So I found some olive oil, anointed myself with it, and then I went into a closet and shut the door. I wanted to be in secret and do it right.

Maybe God smiled when He saw me—but He was with me in those days. When we are fasting, we must not let the slightest hint of it leak out. Only God needs to know. And He who "sees in secret will reward you openly."

The second thing is that fasting must be special. I question if it ought to be done regularly. I don't see fasting as something to be done whether you really need to or not, for example, making a commitment to fast every Friday. I think if it is used that way, it will lose its significance.

Third, as we have seen, fasting must have a purpose. We must know what we want to achieve. It's not like taking vitamins in the general hope that they will do us good. The fourth point is that fasting must be sensible. Some people cannot fast for medical reasons. If, for example, you are a diabetic, then that ought to disqualify you. And we must never fast without drinking a lot of liquids. There are various degrees of fasting. You can cut out one meal or two meals, or fast for a whole day or a number of days. However, anyone seeking to fast for more than two or three days should first seek advice from an experienced Christian minister or counselor.

After a couple of days you start feeling very good. There is nothing spiritual in this. It's merely due to changes in the body chemistry, which is why it is good to fast for physical reasons. So don't think after two days, "Ah—God has spoken to me!" In fact, don't look for any great breakthrough while you are fasting. It can come then, of course, but the results usually come weeks later.

A fifth thing is that fasting must be spontaneous: that is, voluntary and from the heart. In my opinion there could be danger in corporate fasting, for some may be acting reluctantly and under pressure. Another difficulty about corporate fasting is that those who are taking part may be tempted to feel very self-righteous. They may judge those who are not, and ask why they are not joining in. This sort of behavior lets the devil in.

The situation needs to be very urgent before a church calls for a day of prayer and fasting, and if it does happen, nobody must know who is taking part. There might be a case for a group to get together discreetly and covenant to fast, but the members of the group would have to be very careful not to become self-righteous or judgmental.

The next thing I need to say is that fasting must be sacrificial. Isaiah 58 describes people who fasted, but who loved it. The prophet said, "Certainly, on the day of your fast you find your desire" (Isa. 58:3). In the summer of 1984 I was in the Florida Keys. I had a particular burden about decision making, and I fasted for three days. I could have gone out and bonefished while I was fasting. But I didn't because I knew that would have been a mockery. I couldn't fast and go out fishing. No— fasting is a time of sacrifice, and if there is not some element of sacrifice, I question whether the fasting will be honored by the Holy Spirit.

Finally, we must be quite clear about our motives. And we must not have mixed motives. If you want to fast for physical reasons, then say so. But don't say, "I need to lose a little weight and get help about this problem. So I think I'll kill two birds with the one stone and fast."

There is one final point. Could it be that some of us need to practice a different form of fasting? Perhaps we need to abstain from our favorite television program, for example, or fast from judging others? This is what the people of Israel were called to do in Isaiah 58. The people were enjoying fasting, but Isaiah said, "Is not this [rather] the fast that I have chosen: to loose the bonds of wickedness, to undo the heavy burdens...take away... from your midst, the pointing of the finger, and speaking wickedness" (vv. 6, 9). Fasting by itself is no magic answer to our problems. It is only effective when it symbolizes a deep longing for spiritual reality, and it demands a life of holiness and obedience to God. "Then," says God in Isaiah 58:8, "your light shall break forth as the morning, and your healing shall spring forth quickly."

CHAPTER 18

...WITH SINGING

Sing unto the Lord with thanksgiving...

—PSALM 147:7

I N OUR ATTEMPT to discover the quality and components of true worship, our touchstone has been Paul's words in Philippians 3:3: "For we are the circumcision who worship God in the Spirit." We now come to ask, "What about singing? Can it be by the Spirit?" Of course, for most people, worship and singing are synonymous, but we have been seeing that there is much more to worship than singing. Moreover, we have been trying to look at principles first, and in our understanding of worship we are seeking to include only what springs from the impulse of the Spirit. What, then, is the place of singing?

To find out, let's look at the teaching of the Bible.

The first reference to singing in the Bible comes in Exodus 15:1. Israel had just witnessed the wrath of God poured out upon the firstborn of Egypt. But God had said, "When I see the blood, I will pass over you" (Exod. 12:13). So those who had honored Moses's word and had sprinkled blood on door posts and lintel were spared the plague. Then had come the even greater miracle of the crossing of the Red Sea on dry land—probably the most spectacular single miracle in the Old Testament. And now in chapter 15 we find: singing.

From this we can see five things. First, that it is response of gratitude to God. Notice how it is put: "Then Moses and the children of Israel sang this song to the LORD and spoke, saying: 'I will sing to the LORD...'" (v. 1). Never had the people of God been so grateful. They recalled the bitter days under Pharaoh, days they had thought would last forever. But now they were free. Pharaoh could never bother them again; when his army had started after them, the waters had poured back and all had been drowned. They were wonderfully saved from their enemies. No wonder they sang in gratitude to God.

What about us? The people of Israel had something to sing about—but so, surely, does every Christian. Once we were in bondage to sin and on the road to hell. We lived in fear, guilt, and shame. But now we are delivered, and the past will never be held against us. "As far as the east is from the west, so far has He removed our transgressions from us" (Ps. 103:12). Surely every Christian church ought to be a singing church.

The second thing about the singing in Exodus 15 is that the people were rejoicing as they sang: "Then Moses and the children of Israel sang this song to the LORD and spoke, saying: 'I will sing to the LORD, for He has triumphed gloriously! He has thrown the horse and his rider into the sea! The LORD is my strength and song…'" (vv. 1–2). One thing I have learned from all the references I have found to singing in the Bible is that it is synonymous with rejoicing. Look at the Song of Solomon 2:11–12: "For now the winter has past; the rain is over and gone. The flowers appear on the earth; the time of singing has come, and the voice of the turtledove is heard in our land." Or Isaiah 54:1, 4: "Sing, O barren, you who did not bear a child. Break forth into singing and cry aloud, you who did not travail with child. For more are the children of the desolate than the children of the married wife, says the LORD… Do not fear, for you shall not be ashamed." And James says, "Is anyone among you suffering? Let him pray. Is anyone merry? Let him sing psalms" (5:13). When we sing in church, we should sound and look as though we are rejoicing. Our singing is then a testimony to those who are lost. One of the reasons the charismatic movement is growing is that there is such lively and happy singing. When lost people come into these services, they say, "I'm not happy—but these people are." Would that all services caused an unsaved person to say, "I want what these people have."

The third thing about the singing of the children of Israel with Moses is that it was an immediate response to God's extraordinary deliverance. I fear that much of what we sing about is related to events in the distant past. Perhaps when we sing we are remembering the days of our conversion twenty or thirty years ago. But it is hard to get excited about something that happened so long in the past. What has God been doing in our life lately? What happened last week? Or yesterday? Or this morning? If we can think of nothing, then that is perhaps why our singing has turned into another external form. The singing revealed an attitude of reverence, awe, and wonder. The people focused on the greatness of God: "Who is like You, O LORD, among the gods? Who is like You, glorious in holiness, fearful in praises, doing wonders?" (Exod. 15:11). There was simultaneous joy and fear: "The peoples have heard and are afraid; sorrow has taken hold on the inhabitants of Philistia" (v. 14). Reverence that is by the Holy Spirit is not the melancholy, staid attitude which some people call reverence and worship. It affirms the justice and holiness of God and rises spontaneously within us after we have seen God at work. The people of Israel had just seen what God had done to Pharaoh's army—and it had nearly scared them to death. They realized that God is no respecter of persons, and what He had done to the Egyptians He could do to them.

Notice that the Israelites sang their song "*to the* LORD" (Exod. 15:1, emphasis added). When we sing, we are not singing to each other. We are responding to the Lord by singing to Him. And if we were to become keenly aware that God is watching us and listening to us, would it not cause us to take notice and to sing with more reverence, attention, and gratitude, and with less worry about what other people are thinking?

Finally, the singing was a responsibility laid upon the people by Moses. It was the least the people could do. And so it should be with us. As I was preparing this chapter, I found a verse in the Bible which I had never noticed before. It reads: "Also Jehoiada appointed the offices of the house of the LORD by the hand of the priests the Levites, whom David had distributed in the house of the LORD"—and here is the interesting bit—"to offer the burnt offerings of the LORD, as it is written in the law of Moses, with rejoicing and with singing, as it was ordained by David" (2 Chron. 23:18, KJV). Do you see what it is saying here? Singing was not anything new in David's days, but it was so important to David that he got the credit for ordaining it. But David did more than just ordain singing. In those days they did not have a rich hymnody to draw upon. They often had to compose something right on the spot. How many times does David say, "I will sing a new song unto the Lord"? The song of Exodus 15 was a new song. David sang one psalm after another, and they were always new psalms. But many of us just want the same old thing. And we try to cover our steps by saying, "I'm just old-fashioned." But when there is joy, and when the Spirit is coming down, He is always moving us forward. Isaac Watts grew up complaining about the "boring" psalms he had to sing—so his father challenged him to produce something better. And he gave us such hymns as "When I Survey the Wondrous Cross" and "Alas! And Did My Savior Bleed?" Charles Wesley could have said, "Well, we've got Isaac Watts and the psalms." Yet God led him to write six thousand hymns. And John Newton was criticized because he wrote a new hymn every week and taught it to his congregation each Sunday night. We would perhaps not wish to sing *all* that was composed by Watts or Newton or Wesley—just as not *all* that is being composed nowadays is good. But we should be open to the new.

Perhaps you have wondered why it says at the beginning of so many psalms, "To the Chief Musician" (AKJV) or, as the NIV puts it, "For the director of music"? Well, this is because the one hundred fifty psalms in the Bible were originally sung to prescribed music. For example, there was a tune called "Do Not Destroy," which was used for Psalms 57, 58, 59 and 75. (When we get to heaven, we will find out what it sounded like!)

This shows that in those days musicians and singers employed the practice common today of setting new words to an old tune.

The little word *Selah* in the middle of many psalms was originally a direction for the conductor who was leading the instruments, and indicated an interlude where the orchestra would play a little bit before the singing started again.

There is evidence both in Scripture and in the rabbinic sources that the art of singing, particularly singing for the temple, was diligently cultivated. 1 Chronicles 25:6–9 says, "All these were under the direction of their father for the music in the house of the LORD with cymbals, harps, and lyres, for the service of the house of God by decree of the king: Asaph, Jeduthun, and Heman. So the number of them, with their brothers, who were trained in singing to the LORD, all of whom were skillful, was two hundred and eighty-eight. They cast lots for their duties, small and great, teacher and student alike. The first lot fell for Asaph." (And Asaph is often mentioned in the psalms as a chief musician.) So not only was music and singing brought in, but it was not second-class singing. It was to be done skillfully and professionally. There is even a hint in the Talmud (the rabbinic commentary upon Scripture) that a failure to sing correctly annulled the value of the sacrifice. But in any case, this reference shows how seriously singing was taken. If someone was going to sing, they wanted him to sing well. In fact, the training of Levitical singers involved at least five years of intensive preparation.

This indicates that we should take care to sing to the best of our ability. Slovenly, careless, and half-hearted singing does nothing to glorify God. It also shows the important role of a church choir, where those who are gifted in singing can lead the congregation out in worship. To sing in the choir is a responsibility and a calling from God.

A very dear friend of mine pulled out of a larger denomination to start his own reformed church. Overreacting, he made the architect draw up plans that would make it impossible to have a choir in the new church. But after two or three years the singing was so dead and dismal that they found a place for a choir after all.

And working on this chapter I saw something else which I hadn't seen before. In Ephesians 5:19 Paul counsels the people to speak to each other "in psalms, hymns, and spiritual songs, singing and making melody in your heart to the Lord." And in verse 18, Paul says, "Do not be drunk with wine, for that is reckless living. But be filled with the Spirit."

Now in the Greek language they had no punctuation marks. The text just kept on going, which means that these verses ran together. So from that you could ask the question, "Is 'making melody in your heart' the *effect* of being filled with the Spirit, or the *means* of being filled with the Spirit?" Is Paul here asking the people first to be filled with the Spirit, and then to speak to themselves "in psalms...making melody in your heart to the Lord"? Let anyone who is praying to be filled with the Spirit put these two verses together and take Paul seriously. We may want praise to flow from our lives spontaneously, but Isaiah talks of putting on "the garment of praise" (61:3). And the psalmist speaks of offering "sacrifices of joy" (Ps. 27:6). Sometimes we just don't feel like singing. But we have so much to be thankful for that we must just do it. There is even a case for singing in private. Paul says, "Making melody in your heart" (Eph. 5:19). God doesn't expect us all to have great voices. He doesn't care how well we can carry a tune—and some of us couldn't carry a tune in a bucket! But God sees the heart, and the melody is there.

Paul says, "I will sing with the Spirit, and I will sing with the understanding" (1 Cor. 14:15). May God grant us to sing with the Spirit and to sing with the understanding, and above all to sing to Him and to no one else. If every congregation did that, the worship in our churches would take off as it never has before. It would be a testimony to the lost—and God would be glorified.

CHAPTER 19

...WITH MUSIC

Praise Him with the sound of the trumpet; praise Him with the lyre and harp! Praise Him with the tambourine and dancing; praise Him with stringed instruments and flute! Praise Him with loud cymbals; praise Him with the clanging cymbals! Let everything that has breath praise the Lord. Praise the Lord!

—PSALM 150:3–6

I HAVE HAD GREAT joy in working on the material in this chapter, not merely because of the many things I have learned, but because music means so much to me. I have always understood how Martin Luther could say that next to theology, he loved music. My mother made me start taking piano lessons when I was eight years old. I used to protest then at having to practice—but the day came when I was giving concerts. And I developed a love for classical music, particularly the Russian composers. I also learned to play the oboe, and through that discovered Handel. In fact, I could have made playing the oboe my career. Music does something for me at the natural level. Like Saul, who was "refreshed" when David played the harp (1 Sam. 16:23), I know the feeling of being low and having music lift my spirit.

And if there is one thing that I love more than a symphony orchestra, it is a pipe organ. When I first started preaching, I used to dream that someday God would let me be pastor of a church with a pipe organ. Well, I never dreamed that the church would be in London, but I gather that the organ at

Westminster Chapel is one of the three or four finest instruments in London. If music can do something for the spirit at the natural level, how much more ought talented, Spirit-led, Spirit-controlled music lead our spirits out to worship God?

If I have learned anything in the preparation of this chapter, it is that God loves music. Music is of God. After all—He is the one who thought of it. Music appears throughout the Bible, but the first reference to it goes back to Genesis 4:21, where we are told that a man by the name of Jubal was "the father of all those who play the harp and flute."

The last references to music come in the Book of Revelation, where harps are frequently mentioned. According to Revelation, in heaven there will be both singing and instrumental music. This fact should be sufficient to refute any suggestion that the use of musical instruments in church is not biblical.

My father used to tell a story about a Bible study that took place one evening in someone's living room in Kentucky. Suddenly two elderly, saintly women looked at each other and one said, "Do you hear that?"

The other replied, "Yes, isn't it beautiful?" No one else in the room heard anything, but tears filled these two ladies' eyes, for they were hearing music from heaven. We don't know what that will be like, but it will be a sound that will fill us with joy. I like to think that it could be like the sound of a waterfall or the noise of waves hitting the shore, for Jesus's voice is described as "the sound of many waters" (Rev. 1:15).

In the time of Moses, we have the use of trumpets to call the children of Israel together and as a marching signal for the different sections of their camps. Numbers 10:1–2 says, "And the Lord spoke to Moses, saying: Make for yourself two silver trumpets. Of a hammered work you will make them, and you will use them for summoning of the assembly and directing the breaking up of the camps." Trumpets were used to send signals. Verses 5–7 continue, "When you blow an alarm, then the camps that lie on the east will set out. When you blow an alarm the second time, then the camps that lie on the south will set out...

But when the assembly is to be gathered together, you will blow, but you will not sound an alarm."

The concept of music as art was alien to the ancient world. Nowadays some of us go to the symphony simply to listen to the music—but in those days it was an organic part of life from birth to death. Music was essential. In ancient times people thought of music the way we think of flowers. You don't have to have flowers near you all the time, but you can't imagine a world without them. Music was for social merrymaking, for worship, and in war to terrorize the enemy. Judges 7:18–21 says, "When I and all who are with me blow the horn, then you will blow the horns all around the camp and shout, 'For the Lord and for Gideon!'...Then they blew the horns... Every man stood in his place all around the camp, but the men in the camp ran, shouted, and fled." So it was not a matter of art and pleasant listening.

Before the establishment of David's kingdom women played the major part in the performance of music. There was Miriam with her tambourine, Deborah, and the daughter of Jephthah. In 1 Samuel 18:6–7 we read of the incident which so infuriated Saul: "When they came home, as David was returning from slaying the Philistine, the women came out from all cities of Israel to meet King Saul, singing and dancing, with tambourines, with joy, and with musical instruments. The dancing women sang and said, 'Saul has slain his thousands, and David his ten thousands.'"

Up to this time there were no professional musicians as we think of them today. But they began to make an appearance in David's time, and from then on we hear more about men taking the lead in music.

David, the only man in the Bible whom God called "a man after My own heart" (Acts 13:22), loved music. He prescribed it. He wrote it, and he played it. As we saw in the last chapter, singing was ordained by David (2 Chron. 23:18). David polished and refined music and made it an integral part of worship. And the professional musician was a functionary of high rank.

An interesting question is: Where did the Levites who were appointed to be musicians in the time of David get their training? It is thought that they received their instruction from professional musicians from Egypt to Assyria who were invited to Jerusalem in order to train the Israelite musicians and singers. And we do a similar thing today. When we send our children to learn music from professional teachers, we don't know if the teacher is a Christian. We just want the best teaching.

In Old Testament times there were four types of instruments (there are five today). The first category was the idiophone (which we would call percussion), where the instrument's own material produced the tone. In this group were bells, castanets, cymbals, and chimes. In the second category were the aerophones, or wind instruments—the bugle, ram's horn, horn, trumpet, flute, oboe, clarinet, the pipe, bagpipe, and sackbut. In the third group were the membranophones, or instruments for vibration, such as the tambourine, timbrel, and drum. (Today we would class the idiophones and membranophones together, as the percussion.) Finally there were the chordophones—the stringed instruments: harp, lute, psaltery, lyre, dulcimer, and viol. (And today we have electronic music to add to this list.) It is also interesting to note that the harp—David's instrument— was considered the noblest of all. It was the instrument of the aristocracy and was often made of precious woods and metals.

In 1 Chronicles 15 we find a description of the occasion when David brought the ark to Jerusalem. David wanted to get it right this time. He had tried once before and things had gone wrong. Chapter 13 tells how on that first time a man named Uzzah had put out his hand to steady the ark and had been struck dead. And for three months the ark had been left where it was.

On that first occasion, and now on this second occasion, it was assumed that there would be music. Chapter 15:16 says, "Then David told the leaders of the Levites to position their brothers the singers with musical instruments, harps, lyres, and cymbals to resound with joyful songs." It never crossed their minds to celebrate such an important event without music.

We see from 1 Chronicles 15 that music is an aid to worship. Verse 28 says, "So all Israel brought up the ark of the covenant of the Lord with a shout and with the sound of the ram's horn and with trumpets and cymbals, making music on harps and lyres." The instruments led the way so that the singers could find their tune. Psalm 33:1–3 says, "Rejoice in the LORD, O you righteous, for praise is fitting for the upright. Give thanks to the LORD with the harp; make music to Him with an instrument of ten strings. Sing to Him a new song; play an instrument skillfully with a joyful shout." The music enabled the singers to find their place, and it was played skillfully and absolutely correctly.

I have already mentioned the role of a choir in worship. Music can even make or break the atmosphere in a service. I never will forget preaching some years ago in a church that had an organist whose style mirrored a recalcitrant spirit. It was very difficult to sing to his playing. There would be long pauses between some verses, and no pause at all between others and you didn't know which he would do next. It was obviously a way of making the congregation follow him and of drawing attention to himself, and it was a very sad situation.

Someone responsible for leading the singing and music in church needs natural skill, spiritual discernment, and a desire for the glory of God, not for the praise of men. And this is what David was seeking when he "told the leaders of the Levites to position their brothers the singers with musical instruments, harps, lyres, and cymbals to resound with joyful songs" (1 Chron. 15:16).

This brings me to the aim of music. First Chronicles 16:4 says, "And he appointed some of the Levites to minister before the ark of the LORD, to commemorate, to thank, and to praise the LORD God of Israel." Verses 5 and 6 go on: "But Asaph made music with the cymbals. Moreover, Benaiah and Jahaziel the priests sounded trumpets continually [NIV: regularly] before the ark of the covenant of God." And 1 Chronicles 9:33 says, "Now these are the singers, heads of the fathers' houses of the Levites, who stayed in the temple chambers, free from other service, because they were occupied with the work *day and night*." The people considered that *God* wanted to hear music even when Israel slept, for the aim of music was to praise God.

These verses help us to understand other references, such as Psalm 134:1: "Come, bless the LORD, all you servants of the LORD, who by night stand in the house of the LORD." Or Psalm 150: "Praise the LORD! Praise God in His sanctuary... Praise Him with the sound of the trumpet; praise Him with the lyre and harp! Praise Him with the tambourine and dancing; praise Him with stringed instruments and flute!"

The aim of music was to bring glory to God by expressing praise and gratitude. So in Psalm 92 we read: "It is good to give thanks to the LORD, and to sing praises unto Your name, O Most High: to declare forth Your lovingkindness in the morning and Your faithfulness in the night, on a ten-stringed lute and on the harp, and on the lyre with a solemn sound" (vv. 1–3).

From the time of Solomon onwards, music became an accessory to the sacrificial rituals, but only an accessory. Important as the musician was, his music was not seen as an end in itself. An ominous trend in some places today is to make music almost the center of worship. But this should not be. Music is only one part of a service of worship. You cannot worship God without his Word: "It pleased God through the foolishness of preaching to save those who believe" (1 Cor. 1:21).

But if you go to heaven, I hope you like music! God likes it so much that He has even chosen the trumpet as His way of announcing the Second Coming. 1 Corinthians 15:51–52 says, "Listen, I tell you a mystery: We shall not all sleep, but we shall all be changed. In a moment, in the twinkling of an eye, at the last trumpet, for the trumpet will sound, the dead will be raised incorruptible, and we shall be changed." As Paul says in 1 Thessalonians 4:16, "For the Lord Himself will descend from heaven with a shout, with the voice of the archangel, and with the trumpet call of God."

There is coming a day when God is going to sound a trumpet such as this generation or any other generation in the history of the world has never heard, for it will raise the dead. And then singing and music will go on forever and ever in heaven. But until that day comes, thank God for good music—for Spirit-led music—which aids our worship while having as its only aim the glory of God.

CHAPTER 20

...WITH THE WHOLE PERSONALITY

*I urge you therefore, brothers, by the mercies of
God, that you present your bodies as a living
sacrifice, holy, and acceptable to God, which is your
reasonable service of worship. Do not be conformed
to this world, but be transformed by the renewing
of your mind, that you may prove what is the
good and acceptable and perfect will of God.*

—ROMANS 12:1–2

WHEN WE SPEAK of the impulse of the Spirit, we are in some sense talking about feelings. I admit this is dangerous, because feelings can lead people to do strange things. This impulse may take the form of an insight that is based upon accumulated knowledge. It may be a suspicion that is based upon knowledge experienced. But the impulse of the Spirit, when obeyed, always leads to a feeling of immense peace.

One of the most helpful verses in this connection is Romans 14:19. In the NIV it reads: "Let us therefore make every effort to do what leads to peace and to mutual edification." The proof that the impulse of the Spirit lies behind our feeling that we ought to do something is the peace that obedience brings. This verse applies not only to a situation where tensions among people need to be defused but also to our own inmost feelings. God will never lead us to do what violates our conscience. When I am really following Him, I will have an inner ease that testifies to the fact that I have been true to myself. "To thine own self be true," said Shakespeare.[1] Romans 14:19 agrees! When a lack of inner peace—a heaviness or feeling of oppression—results from obeying any impulse, I know that impulse was not of God.

The reason why following the impulse of the Spirit is potentially dangerous is, first, because immature people may surmise the Spirit's impulse and be utterly, ridiculously, and sadly wrong. An example of this is a horror story from near Chattanooga, Tennessee. Many years ago a sincere Christian lady felt she was led of the Holy Spirit to take literally Jesus's words, "If your right hand causes you to sin, cut it off" (Matt. 5:30). Her husband came home from work one day to find she had cut off her arm with a hatchet. It was a scandal in that area, and many people never got over the trauma.

Overly conscientious people, driven by a feeling of guilt, may seek to offset a foolish wrong action by doing something that they think is the will of God. Someone may imagine that he is feeling the impulse of the Spirit when all he is doing is making a human effort to atone for a past failure. Sometimes people think that if they go into full-time Christian work, it will make what they did look better or justify it.

Another danger is that a zealous Christian, who is anxious to see God work, may project upon God a particular idea or feeling, and then say that God is leading him or her to do it. I may call something the will of God when it's not the Spirit's impulse but my own wish.

However, these dangers should not make us reject one of the most common assumptions in the Bible—that God made us with the capacity to grasp His leading. This inbuilt capacity that God has given us is one of the means by which God communicates to us what He is feeling. It is because of this, for example, that we experience a sense of guilt and shame. When Adam and Eve sinned, they suddenly knew they were naked and began to clothe themselves with fig leaves. This sense of guilt came from their awareness of God's attitude to sin.

It is the Holy Spirit who convicts of sin, and the only way a person will ever be converted is when the Spirit comes down. The Spirit brings home to us that we have been doing wrong. The Spirit makes us conscious of a grieved holy God.

God wants to communicate with us not just at an intellectual level. I'm touching now on a problem many of us have. It's easy to think that the only stimulation that matters is cerebral brilliance or depth. But God wants to communicate with our whole being—our emotions and senses as well as our minds.

If we suppress genuine, Spirit-led feelings, we put out the Spirit's fire. 1 Thessalonians 5:19 says, "Do not quench the Spirit." The ISV says: "Do not put out the Spirit's fire." Why does Paul say that? He's talking about rejoicing evermore, praying without ceasing, giving thanks in everything. Then he says, "Do not quench the Spirit. Do not despise prophecies" (vv. 19–20). It is because we all have a fear of things getting out of hand. Just as there are those who are afraid to believe in justification by faith because of the fear of lawlessness, so also there are those who want things to be done in rigid order because of the danger of fanaticism. These people are in danger of quenching the Spirit.

However, in the next verse Paul says, "Examine all things. Firmly hold onto what is good" (v. 21). We are to use our minds. God wants us to have our heads screwed on. We are to be harmonious, whole, and balanced people.

The events of the first Palm Sunday provide an illustration of the right way to worship. Here were hundreds praising the Lord Jesus as He came down from the Mount of Olives on His way to Jerusalem. The feelings of the people exploded on this Palm Sunday. They were full of expectancy and excitement. As we saw in Chapter 7, there is worship in expectancy. Donald Grey Barnhouse once said, "While we wait, we can worship." The prelude itself is to be enjoyed. It's like the hors d'oeuvres or an appetizer at the beginning of a meal.

The people were able to express their feelings. Luke writes: "The whole crowd of the disciples began to rejoice and praise God with loud voices for all the mighty works that they had seen" (19:37). They had heard about Jesus. Many had seen what He had done, and they began to talk together. One said, "He changed my life." Another said, "You should talk to my sister. She was paralyzed." And another: "Let me tell you what happened to me." There were reports all over the place. On this day they thought it was all coming together. At long last what each of the people felt instinctively and individually was coalescing into one great, climactic event. They let themselves go.

Real worship takes place when we are unafraid to express what we feel. There's nothing that leads to greater pain than repressed feelings. Repression is a defense mechanism. We can't face up to what we feel, so we deny it, sometimes unconsciously, involuntarily. But we don't get rid of something by repressing it. It goes down into our subconscious and comes out later as high blood pressure or mental illness or something else.

We need to learn to express our feelings, at least to ourselves and to God. We need to admit to ourselves what we really think and feel. For example, perhaps we weren't honest about our feelings a year ago, but now we can say, "This is the way I really felt. I see it now. I wish I had seen it then and been true to myself at that time.

Worship ought to bring us to the point where we can be honest right now. We never need to repress what we feel when we are around Jesus. He will never scold us for our honesty. It doesn't mean we are right, but if we are being honest, He can help us and bring us to see where we are wrong and to face the truth.

We may envy the people's exuberance on Palm Sunday. We may say, "I wish I could do that. I just can't get excited like this. They shouted out loud, but that's not my nature. How could they do it?"

There's only one answer. Jesus was right there. When Jesus is there, you forget everybody else and let yourself go. Possibly the highest goal in worship is simply not to be self-conscious but only conscious of Jesus. Then we will express our feelings!

On Palm Sunday the people's feelings were spontaneous.

There was no script, no director, no order of worship. Jesus didn't say, "Matthew, on my signal you come and read the twenty-third Psalm." The people took over. John's account says, "On the next day a great crowd that had come to the feast heard that Jesus was coming to Jerusalem. They took branches of palm trees, and went out to meet Him, and cried out: 'Hosanna! [that is, Salvation]'" (12:12–13).

But it wasn't a coup. They weren't trying to get control. Some church leaders stamp on any spontaneous expression of feelings because they want to build their empire and are paranoid that somebody is going to try and take over. Was Jesus upset? Did He disown this demonstration? Here He was riding down the Mount of Olives on the donkey and people were spreading their clothes out in front of it and waving and shouting. Was Jesus saying, "Don't do that. Stop it"? Of course not. Praise was due to Him.

When anybody gets excited over Jesus, you must let them. Someone may get carried away, and you may want to say, "Isn't that going over the top? How embarrassing!" But it's not bothering the Lord. It's you who's got the problem. Some people criticized on that first Palm Sunday. Luke 19:39 says, "Some of the Pharisees from the crowd said to Him, 'Teacher, rebuke Your disciples.'" People like that will always be around. When revival comes, there will be those stationed around taking notes to report what's going on. But Jesus will never rebuke fervent worship. Look what He said to those Pharisees: "I tell you, if these should be silent, the stones would immediately cry out" (v. 40).

That was Palm Sunday—look at how much more fervent the worship was on Easter Day. In Matthew 28:9 we read: "As they went to tell His disciples, suddenly Jesus met them, saying, 'Greetings!' They came and *took hold of His feet* and worshipped Him" (emphasis added).

The two Marys had just discovered the empty tomb, and the angel had said, "Go quickly and tell His disciples that He has risen from the dead" (Matt. 28:7). As they were rushing to find the disciples, Jesus met them on the way. He came to where they were, and they weren't expecting this. It was an unplanned meeting. The result was spontaneous worship: they worshipped with their bodies, on their faces on the ground. We know this because Matthew writes that they came and held Him by the feet.

What about the subject of worshipping with our bodies? I believe that when it is spontaneous and not contrived, this too is glorifying to God. In Chapter 19 we were looking at how David brought the ark to Jerusalem. David became so excited by the atmosphere provided by the singing and the instruments that he began to dance. The Hebrew says that he made "a swirl" around the ark. David's dancing was spontaneous; he wasn't taking directions from a choreographer. Michal's reaction shows that it was unexpected and unrehearsed: when she saw him getting carried away, we are told that "she despised him in her heart" (1 Chron. 15:29). Unspiritual people often despise those who really enjoy themselves in the Lord.

When dancing is a spontaneous response to the glory and love of God, it does bring praise to Him. But it must be spontaneous and not contrived. Dancing as a planned so-called art form, I fear, draws more attention to the performance than to the adoration of God.

I preach with my body, especially when I feel free in the Spirit. We must be free to express our feelings with our bodies. In their joy and love for Him the two Marys held onto Jesus. There's a place for hugging in our Christian life. I'm sure people hugged each other in the New Testament. The "holy kiss" (Rom. 16:16; 1 Cor. 16:20; 2 Cor. 13:12; 1 Thess. 5:26; 1 Pet. 5:14) was probably a hug or kiss on the cheek.

A man in our church told me that when I once told everyone to take the hand of the person they were sitting with, he looked at the person next to him and thought the man would resent it. "But," he said, "I hesitated and then put my hand out to him and he took it. When it was time to break, he held on a little longer and I could see that he appreciated a feeling of acceptance." There are some people who just want to feel accepted, and a touch can mean more than many words.

Jesus said to the two Marys: "Do not be afraid. Go tell My brothers to go to Galilee, and there they will see Me" (Matt. 28:10). Jesus called His followers "brothers." My parents hugged each other, and they hugged me. I hug my son and my daughter. When we are Christians, we belong to each other: we are a family, so there is a right time to hug. But if it is not a spontaneous expression of Christian love and compassion, and if it is not mutually edifying, hugging is wrong and could be counterproductive. There are those who don't want this, and that is all right. We must be straight with each other and respect each other's feelings.

Another mark of the Easter Day worship was that the two Marys were filled with very deep and conflicting emotions: "They departed quickly from the tomb with fear and great joy" (Matt. 28:8). The NIV says, "Afraid yet filled with joy." They felt simultaneous joy and fear. This sometimes happens. In Acts 2:43 we read, "Fear came to every soul." Three verses later it says, "And continuing daily with one mind in the temple, and breaking bread from house to house, they ate their food with *gladness* and simplicity of heart" (emphasis added).

Often we experience mixed feelings about something. This can happen at a purely natural level. We may come to church, for example, feeling hopeful or excited, and also with a natural fear and timidity. There may also be a residual unbelief that results in fear, or fear as a result of a satanic attack. This sort of fear is not from God, for Paul wrote to Timothy: "For God has not given us the spirit of fear, but of power, and love, and self-control" (2 Tim. 1:7).

There may also be joy at the natural level. We may come to church feeling good because everything is going well. Maybe the sun is out, or we've had a pay raise, good news, or a letter from home, and we feel great. There's nothing wrong with this. Thank God for it. But it's not to be confused with spiritual joy.

God was the source of the mixed joy and fear felt by the two Marys. They didn't know what it all meant. But even though they were scared nearly to death, they were filled with happiness. They knew that something wonderful was taking place. I am talking here about one of the grandest, most magnificent experiences known to man: the fear of God, the sense of awe because we can't explain it, but the tremendous joy and almost overwhelming sense of excitement because we know God is up to something.

But someone may say, "That's all very well, but they saw Jesus with their own eyes. If I could see Jesus with my very eyes, then I too might fall at His feet and hold onto them."

It is very easy for us to think that, if only we could see Jesus, we would believe and worship. Yet when we look at Jesus's resurrection appearances, we see something extraordinary. Matthew writes: "When they saw Him, they worshipped Him. *But some doubted*" (Matt. 28:17, emphasis added).

How could this have happened? How could anybody doubt when they are seeing? "Seeing is believing," it is often said, but here were some who saw but still doubted.

Yet it is not surprising when you stop to consider what we have been learning about worship. Philippians 3:3 says that we worship by the Spirit of God. It is the Spirit who reveals Jesus. And today the Spirit gives us the eyes to see as those first believers saw with their physical eyes. The more we have of the Spirit, the more we will see and feel what they felt.

When Jesus went away, He sent another "Comforter" (Greek: *paraclete*, which literally means "one who comes alongside"). The Holy Spirit simply brings us right back to the way it was when Jesus was here.

Conversely, no matter how much one may see with one's eyes, if the Holy Spirit is not present, one sees nothing with one's spirit, and there is no worship.

The corollary of this is that relying on sight to create a sense of worship in our services has its dangers. Without the Spirit there is the likelihood of idolatry, of worshipping a "graven image." C. H. Spurgeon used to say that the less we have of the Spirit, the more we will need to see physical things to inspire us. On the other hand, when we truly worship by the impulse of the Spirit, there is little need to have a lot of visual aids.

Even when Moses saw the burning bush, he was not allowed to get very close or look for very long. The phenomenon he sighted was transcended by the Word of God: "Moses, Moses... Do not approach here. Remove your sandals from off your feet, for the place on which you are standing is holy ground" (Exod. 3:4–5). God may accommodate us with what is visible, as in the bread and wine at the Lord's Supper, but the end is not in seeing with our physical eyes, but "discerning the Lord's body" by faith (1 Cor. 11:29).

The Holy Spirit gave Peter the vision on the roof in Caesarea, but again, what was seen was upstaged by what was heard: "What God has cleansed, do not call common" (Acts 10:15). Therefore, even a vision, if one be so blessed by God, is not an end in itself, but the means by which the Word of God is magnified.

Last summer I came in from a day's bonefishing in the Florida Keys. As I came away, I looked back towards the sea. It was so beautiful. The sky was blue; the clouds were white and fluffy; the wind was gentle. I felt that God was saying to me, "How do you like what I have done for you today in providing this for you?" I felt that so often we take God's creation for granted, and that God wanted to be noticed and thanked for what He has done at the natural level. Since then I have made it a point to be thankful and worship God for His creation.

Yet even creation, with all its beauty, only reveals the glory and love of God to the man who is taught by the Spirit of God. Some people see only indifference and cruelty in the created world.

The ability to see with our spirit what God is doing and to hear with our inward ear what God is saying is God's gift to us. Some people can see more quickly than others what God is up to. It's not necessarily that the others are being rebellious or hostile or digging in their heels; they are just sincerely not sure. Does Jesus slap their wrist? Does He get on to them and say,

"Come on. Shame on you"? No. He calls attention to what He is in Himself: "All authority has been given to Me in heaven and on earth" (Matt. 28:18). He just continues to speak. All we must do is continue to give all our attention to Jesus. C. H. Spurgeon once said: "Look to Jesus and a dove will fly into your heart, but look to the dove and it will fly away." And then we must obey Him with our mind, and will and feelings. This quality of attention and obedience is what worshipping with the whole personality means.

And in the act of obedience doubts and fears often slip away, and we are filled with joy and trust and a true spirit of worship. A lot of people say, "I can't start doing what God tells me to do because I'm waiting to be filled with the Spirit." Start doing it and God will fill you! The two Marys met Jesus as they obeyed the angel. As we give our whole selves to Jesus in obedience, He meets us. And then we truly know what it means to worship in spirit and in truth.

CHAPTER 21

WORSHIP AND TRADITION

Where the Spirit of the Lord is, there is liberty.

—2 CORINTHIANS 3:17

A FEW SUMMERS AGO, when I was on holiday in Florida, I was invited to preach one Sunday morning at the Coral Ridge Presbyterian Church in Fort Lauderdale. It was a very traditional service. Everything was very formal, and we marched in with the choir down the center aisle. I was also wearing a robe.

Later in the afternoon I flew to Bimini in the Bahamas, where I planned to do some fishing on Monday. But that Sunday evening I fulfilled an engagement to preach at the church of the Rev. Sammy Ellis (who used to be known as Bonefish Sam). At that service I didn't even have a tie—I think I was wearing a sports shirt. And of the thirty or so people there, I was the only white man.

Two such opposite experiences and traditions in one day, but God was in both. God used me in that morning service—I received a number of letters about the sermon I preached. And in that little service in Bimini, while we were on our knees praying in the utmost informality, I had an insight into the text on which I was to preach (Hebrews 13:8, "Jesus Christ the same yesterday, and today, and forever") that gave me a perspective on Jesus which I never got over. I also preached to that small congregation with unusual power.

It could be argued from this story that nothing is more irrelevant than tradition. The two services were quite different, and yet God was as powerfully present in the one as in the other. This is something we must always keep in mind.

The atmosphere in our churches, the way we shape our services—even our theology—are all formed by tradition. The whole of Western Christianity is shaped by the fact that our heritage goes back to the Latin Fathers (for example, St. Augustine), and comes up through Thomas Aquinas and Anselm, Luther and Calvin.

If you go to the Soviet Union, where the theology derives from the Greek Fathers, you will find a vastly different tradition and different insights. There was no Reformation in Eastern Christianity, which means that Russian Orthodoxy has been the formative influence on worship in the Soviet Union today.

If we in the West were asked, "What would you reply if God were to say to you, 'Why should I let you into heaven?'" we would probably answer: "Because Jesus died on the cross for my sins." But if we were to ask that question among evangelicals in the Soviet Union, we would probably get the reply, "Because Jesus was raised from the dead." In Eastern Europe the emphasis is on the resurrection.

God has His elect scattered all over the world from all theological traditions.

This word *tradition* means "a handing down of opinions." In our New Testament it is used to translate the Greek word *paradosis*, from the verb *paradidomi*, which means not so much "hand down" as "hand over." The word itself is neutral: it can be good or bad. Nothing can help worship as much as tradition, and equally, nothing can hurt worship as much as tradition.

When the apostle Paul used the word, it was almost always in a positive sense. In 1 Corinthians 11:2 the Greek is translated in the Authorized Version as "ordinances," but it means "tradition": "Now I praise you, brethren, that ye remember me in all things, and keep the ordinances, as I delivered them to you." (That is, "as I handed them over to you".) And in 1 Corinthians 15:3–4 Paul writes, "For I delivered to you first of all that which I also received: how Christ died for our sins according to the

Scriptures, was buried, rose again the third day according to the Scriptures." This was the most ancient tradition of the church—and Paul was affirming it. And he affirmed it again in 2 Thessalonians 2:15, where he says, "Therefore, brothers, stand firm and hold the traditions which you have been taught, whether by word or by our letter." In chapter 3 of the same book he says, "...withdraw yourselves from every brother who walks in idleness and not according to the tradition that he received from us" (v. 6).

When he used this word, Paul meant the true teachings of Jesus passed on from the apostles to the believers in the early Church.

But Jesus used the word in rather a different way, and it is this negative aspect that I want to concentrate on. Matthew 15:3 says, "Why do you also violate the commandment of God by your tradition?" And verse 6 says, "So you have made the commandment of God of no effect by your tradition." Now here Jesus was addressing the Pharisees, who had made the mistake of elevating their traditions to the level of Holy Scripture. As a result they could no longer distinguish between what they practiced and what the Word of God actually taught. Human tradition can be both blinding and binding. It blinds us from seeing things objectively, and it binds us to wrong interpretations.

Now just what was this tradition? It was the Jewish oral law, the oral tradition passed on by word of mouth until eventually someone said, "We'd better write this up." So we have such documents as the Mishnah and the Talmud.

The Mishnah comprises the written collection of Jewish laws that had been preserved orally since the time of Ezra (about 450 BC) and took its final form early in the third century AD. In AD 200-500 Rabbinic comments on the Mishnah were collected to form the Gemara. The Mishnah and Gemara, along with a collection of legal precepts (the Halacha) and nonlegal interpretations of these (the Haggadah) were put together to form the Talmud, dating from the sixth century AD, which all orthodox Jews now have to obey.

In this way traditions were turned into dogma that had to be believed and became the equivalent of Scripture. The same thing has happened in the West with the Roman Catholic Church. The lighting of candles, the idea of purgatory, the concept of the worship of Mary—these were all at one point innovations but were subsequently turned into dogma. The Council of Trent of 1545 did in fact equate tradition with Scripture.

But Protestants are not free of this danger. We must be careful not to do the same, for example, with our Westminster Confession of Faith, the Thirty-Nine Articles—or whatever theological confession we affirm.

"Well," you may ask, "what on earth does this have to do with worship?" The answer to this is—a great deal. In Matthew 15:9 Jesus quoted from Isaiah: "In vain they do worship Me, teaching as doctrines the precepts of men" (29:13). So we see that the equating of human tradition with Scripture can lead to defective worship, what the Authorized Version calls "vain worship."

We all feel good in church when there are things around us with which we are familiar. But we must beware. It may be that we are merely feeling "at home" in a certain tradition. We may like the tone of voice used in the prayer. We may be used to "the hoil," as they say in Wales, or "the holy tone" as we say back in the hills of Kentucky. We may like an elaborate set-up at the altar or, if you come from Tennessee, prefer a simple wooden rail where people can go and kneel. Reformed churches have their pulpits in the center. Some people just have a Bible in the center or have the pulpit off to the side because they think the Eucharist is the center of the worship. All this is merely tradition, and the Spirit of God is not necessarily present in any of it.

What was wrong with the worship of the Pharisees? The first thing is that it was provincial. Matthew 15:1 says, "Then scribes and Pharisees who were *from Jerusalem* came to Jesus" (emphasis added). They had come all the way to Galilee, and they wanted to superimpose Jerusalem on Galilee. They were saying, in effect, "We do it this way in Jerusalem. Why don't you do it that way up here?" If you think provincially, you can only see how things are done in a certain area.

But secondly, the worship of the Pharisees was parochial. Now to be *parochial* means "to be narrow-minded, to feel that certain things are all-important, to the exclusion of wider issues." Matthew 15:2 says, "Why do Your disciples violate the tradition of the elders? For they do not wash their hands when they eat bread." Being parochial is taking one doctrine and making everything revolve around that. If we come to a church wanting to know what the members of that church believe about baptism, or the sovereignty of God, or the baptism of the Spirit before we make up our mind to listen, then we are being a bit parochial.

Look at what had been going on just before the Pharisees asked this question. Matthew 14:35–36 says, "And when the men of that place recognized Him, they sent word to all the surrounding country and brought to Him all who were sick, and begged Him that they might only touch the hem of His garment. And as many as touched it were made perfectly well." People were being healed of diseases of all kinds, and you can imagine the talk there must have been. But the Pharisees were totally unimpressed. All they could do was ask a question about washing your hands. There is nothing in the Bible that says you must wash your hands before you eat. There's certainly nothing wrong with doing it, but it cannot be insisted upon as the infallible Word of God. When the Pharisees insisted on it, their source was not the Bible but the tradition of the elders.

We find the same thing in John 9. Jesus healed a blind man and the Pharisees' reaction was, "This Man is not from God, because He does not keep the Sabbath day" (v. 16). Parochial thinking almost always leads to being judgmental.

I never will forget the story told to me by a British preacher, a friend of mine, who made a trip to America. He stopped first in West Virginia, and during the week he was there his Christian hosts frequently lamented those professing Christians who smoked or drank.

He then moved on to Grand Rapids, Michigan, which is about ninety percent Dutch, and the center of Reformed Calvinism. Here they have what they call the "glorious doctrine of Christian Liberty." He was met by their new host, who was smoking a cigar, and when they got to the house, they were offered a whiskey. But at the end of a Sunday in Grand Rapids they were driving down the road after church when my friend saw a Howard Johnson's restaurant and said, "Oh, I just love their ice-cream!"

There was a silence, but their host pulled over and they all went in. Across the table my friend said, "I know there is something wrong."

The man replied, "Well—this is the Sabbath, and we never buy ice cream on the Sabbath."

My friend said to his wife when they got home, "You know, everybody has got to have something that they are against. I wonder what it is with us."

The worship of the Pharisees was not only provincial and parochial—it was people worship. "Why do Your disciples violate the tradition of the elders?" they asked (Matt. 15:2). At bottom, they worshipped people. Those who started their traditions may have been good, serious, and learned men. They may have been responsible men—but they were only men. All man-made traditions have a beginning in men. Great men tend to have strong views, and they will emphasize certain things. And because they also often have strong personalities, they influence their followers to accept their views. But this is only people worship.

In Matthew 15 we also see that the Pharisees' worship was legalistic—which means a preoccupation with the letter of the law at the expense of the spirit. The Pharisees were so anxious to get every tiny detail right that they ended up with over six hundred laws that modified and explained the simple commandments of the Bible. The result was a distortion of God's Law. They hid behind their interpretations and ended up breaking the very Law they venerated. So Jesus said to them, "For God commanded, 'Honor your father and mother,' and, 'He who speaks evil of father or mother, let him be put to death.' But you say, 'Whoever shall say to his father or his mother, "What you would have profited from me is a gift to God," will be free from honoring his father or his mother.' So you have made the commandment of God of no effect by your tradition" (Matt. 15:4–6).

Finally, their worship was parrot-like; it was worship by rote, by language only. They said the right things, but look at verses 7 and 8, "You hypocrites, Isaiah well prophesied of you, saying: 'These people draw near to Me with their mouth, and honor Me with their lips, but their heart is far from Me.'"

Churches that follow a liturgical pattern of worship are particularly prone to this danger (though a liturgical service is not necessarily bad, as I will try to show in the next chapter). The prayers may be good and solid, the hymns brilliant; everything may be in good taste and theologically sound; the beauty of the language may give you a happy feeling: but if it is just words, it is spiritually useless.

A minister friend of mine was trying to win a prominent lawyer to his church, and finally the man agreed to come to hear him preach. So my friend worked doubly hard on his sermon, and after the service was over, thought, "I've really done it!" And he couldn't wait to get the lawyer's reaction.

The man said, "I've got a book in my office with every word of your sermon in it. Come round tomorrow morning and I'll show it to you."

Well, my friend hardly slept that night. Nine o'clock the next morning found him at the office.

The lawyer handed him a dictionary and said, "Words, preacher—just words."

Yet that is what some people want—as if the words can somehow do the work of worship for them. They should heed the warning of the apostle Paul: "Having a form of godliness, but denying its power" (2 Tim. 3:5).

How do we know that in our worship we ourselves are not

bound and blinded by tradition? The first step is by seeing that there is no such thing as one single right tradition. For what may be right for one may be wrong for someone else. We must also realize that it doesn't take any spirituality at all to uphold a tradition—however valid it maybe. There are three kinds of people—tradition takers, tradition breakers, and tradition makers. The first have no discernment—they simply accept everything as it is. Someone may be converted in a charismatic church and a week later be holding their hands up in the air. Well, it didn't take any great spirituality to do that. Equally, those of us who have never done such a thing in our whole lives are not thereby being spiritual. It is simply that we cannot conceive of ever doing it.

Tradition breakers, too, may not be spiritual. They may just want to be rebellious. As for the tradition maker, he needs to be aware that he is going to leave a legacy that may have to be broken by the next generation. It may only have been valid for one particular set of needs.

The real question we ought to ask is not, "Is our tradition right?" but, "How do we know that our tradition is not wrong?"

Three answers come out in Matthew 15. We know that our tradition is not wrong, first, if it promotes love. The Pharisees' legalistic traditions were right against love: "For God commanded, 'Honor our father and mother'" (v. 4). Love never condones an excuse for setting aside our duty to man. So whether we have banjo-playing or drums or an organ or no music at all—if our tradition promotes love, it is not wrong.

Secondly, if it promotes life-giving heart-worship, then it is not wrong. If someone comes into our service filled with fear and in bondage and is set free, then we are not wrong. "Where the Spirit of the Lord is, there is liberty" (2 Cor. 3:17).

And finally, we know we are not wrong if our tradition promotes conviction of sin. The Pharisees did not have a clue about sin. Everything was external—they thought washing the hands was a mark of good worship. But Jesus said to them, "That which goes into the mouth does not defile a man, but that which comes out of the mouth, this defiles a man...But those things which proceed out of the mouth come from the heart, and they defile the man. For out of the heart proceed evil thoughts, murders, adulteries, sexual immorality, thefts, false witness, and blasphemies. These are the things which defile a man. But to eat with unwashed hands does not defile a man" (Matt. 15:11, 18–20). Worship that is by the Spirit leads inevitably to a sense of sin, insight, and a changed life, which results in holiness.

We do not want to be tradition takers, tradition breakers, or tradition makers. We only want to be sure that our tradition, whatever it is, is not wrong. Let us therefore allow the Holy Spirit to set the standard because what we want is worship that touches the heart and changes lives. There is no value in anything else.

CHAPTER 22

WORSHIP AND LITURGY

*"When you come together...Let all
things be done for edification."*

—1 CORINTHIANS 14:26

A
LTHOUGH IT IS an oversimplification, one can say that there are two basic styles of worship: liturgical and non-liturgical. In liturgical worship the service is taken from a worship book, such as the Book of Common Prayer. The structure of the service and the individual responses, prayers, and readings suggested in the book are all followed.

I confess that in the past I have been very suspicious of this form of worship. I have always called to mind 2 Corinthians 3:17: "Where the Spirit of the Lord is, there is liberty," and have felt that liturgy must mean the opposite of liberty.

But I think I was wrong in my attitude, for I have come to see that there are degrees of structure. Following a planned service can simply mean deciding at which point the collection is to be taken. At the other extreme, it can mean sticking to a rigid order of service with no possibility of variation. I have also seen that some people need this second type of service. Recently, I was talking to a lady whose husband, a minister, had left her and given up his church. She said to me, "I made my way one day to an Anglican church. I needed a liturgical worship, where I knew every Sunday would be the same and there would be no surprises.

The word *liturgy* comes from a Greek word *leitourgias* or *leitourgos*, which, in the Authorized Version, is almost always translated "minister" or "ministry." This word is used twice in Hebrews 8. In verse 2 it refers to "a minister in the sanctuary" (*leitourgos*). And in verse 6 the reference is to the "more excellent ministry" (*leitourgias*) of Jesus. The word means "serving people," but it can mean "serving God," and often means ministering to people through the worship of God, for example, in Romans 15:27, where Paul says, "For if the Gentiles have been partakers of their spiritual things, they also ought to minister [*leitourgesai*] to them in material things."

There is also the reference to Zechariah the priest, father of John the Baptist, of whom it is said, "As soon as the days of his service [*leitourgias*] were fulfilled, he departed to his own home" (Luke 1:23).

In order to prepare this chapter, I have studied the origin and development of liturgy in New Testament times and through church history to the present day, and I have concluded that there is no such thing as non-liturgical worship. It is a myth to think there is. Every church has its own identifiable liturgy. It takes one form in the Church of England and another in the Roman Catholic Church. The Pentecostals have their liturgy, and the charismatics have theirs.

In Chapter 21 I described how I preached one summer for Coral Ridge Presbyterian Church in Fort Lauderdale, where we wore robes and walked behind the choir down the center aisle. The opening hymn was chosen to fit the time it would take us to reach our places. At the end of the last verse there I was already in the pulpit. I knew also when I must finish preaching.

That evening I preached in Bimini with Bonefish Sam in his freestyle service. Now he would claim that they did not follow a liturgy. But the first thing Sam did that night when he came into the pulpit was say, "Praise the Lord!" And the people all replied, "Praise the Lord!" Then he said, "Say, thank You, Jesus!" And everyone said, "Thank You, Jesus." He did it that night, and he will do it tonight and again next week! That's just as liturgical as the church I was at in the morning.

In my own church we only vaguely follow the church calendar. But nobody would be happy if I were to preach on "God's judgment and AIDS" on Christmas morning. Or if on Easter Sunday morning I preached on "The wise men following the star."

Within our free church services we feel that a more formal liturgy is more appropriate on some occasions than others. The Lord's Supper follows a liturgy that Jesus himself introduced. Many churches follow a written order of service and use set prayers and responses for baptismal services. At a funeral service certain scriptures are normally read, and at the graveside we repeat the words, "Ashes to ashes, dust to dust." The wedding service is largely liturgical, as are services dedicating babies to God.

Liturgy was God's idea from the beginning. The Law was total liturgy, yet the giving of the Law was from God. The Law is in three parts: moral, civil, and ceremonial. The moral law is the Ten Commandments. The civil law showed how the people of Israel should govern themselves and get on with each other. And the ceremonial law set out in detail how to worship God. In Exodus, Leviticus, Numbers, and Deuteronomy, for example, there are careful descriptions of the tabernacle, the altar, the show bread, the candles, and the incense; the movements of the priest on the Day of Atonement are carefully prescribed.

Jesus fulfilled the whole Law—ceremonial, civil, and moral—by His life and by His death. We in turn fulfill it in two ways. One is by substitution. None of us could ever totally keep the Law, but Jesus kept it perfectly. Christ is our righteousness and our sanctification, our wisdom and our redemption. In Christ all of us perfectly fulfill the Law.

We fulfill the Law also by walking in the Spirit, for if we walk in the Spirit, we will not obey the lusts of the flesh. This is why worship is to be by the Spirit.

The question for us, therefore, is: Does worship in the Spirit negate the need for all structure and all liturgy in our personal lives and in our church services?

I would say that the answer is, "Certainly not." In the chapter on prayer we have already seen that the presence of the Holy Spirit in the early church did not prevent Peter and John going to the temple to pray at a set time of prayer (Acts 3:1). Even where there is a great measure of the Spirit, we need a place and a time to pray. Some people fancy they are so spiritual that they can just read the Bible as they feel led and pray when they are in the mood. But these people are shallow and know little of the real impulse of the Spirit. We must never think that we can outgrow structure in our own lives. We need a disciplined Bible-reading plan, and not one of us can afford to pray for less than thirty minutes a day,

What are the advantages of liturgy and structure in a church worship service? I would like to name five, although there may well be more. The first is that it enables people to know when to start and where to meet.

Second, it sometimes helps people with no Christian background.

Third, it ensures that worship has theological content. Christians who know nothing but a completely unstructured style of worship tend to be theologically and spiritually starved. Some churches would possibly benefit from using set prayers. We have a rich heritage of prayers written by theologically-minded, godly people. These prayers would bring far greater blessing than the endless diet of repetitive, superficial chorus singing that in some churches virtually takes up the entire service.

A fourth advantage of liturgy is that it provides a measure of blessing if the minister or preacher is not leading the worship in the Spirit. We may sometimes think, "I'm not going this morning, the preacher is not a man of God." But liturgies, prayers, and hymns normally have been written by men of God, and God can speak through them, no matter who is leading the service. They also help us to avoid getting into extremes, such as the Quaker idea of just sitting and waiting in the service for the Spirit to move the people.

Another point is that, in these days of waiting for revival, when we often don't feel like praying, it is helpful to be able to fall back on liturgy and structure. Paul said, "Be ready in season and out of season" (2 Tim. 4:2).

A final advantage of liturgy is that it provides a promise that the service will come to an end. And if the Spirit does not come down in the kind of power one wishes for, it is good to know that the service will stop!

What I have been saying is that God can own a prescribed worship just as much as He can own a prescribed sermon. I myself don't come to the pulpit unprepared. I know most of what I'm going to say before I come—though I may think of some of my stories or illustrations as I go along. I don't read my sermons, but would it matter if I did? In his most powerful sermon, "Sinners in the Hands of an Angry God," preached in Enfield, Connecticut in 1741, Jonathan Edwards took as his text the words from Deuteronomy 32:35: "Their foot shall slide in due time: for the day of their calamity is at hand" (KJV). Before he had finished speaking, five hundred strong men were found outside holding onto tree trunks to keep from falling into hell. Inside they were holding on to the pews, so great was the sense of the Spirit's presence. Yet Edwards had poor eyesight and was forced to hold his manuscript up to his eyes as he read.

We need to be aware of the difference between the liturgical and the sacramental. When we talk of a service being "liturgical," we are referring to the outward form only. A liturgical service has no power to transform those who take part. Without the presence of the Holy Spirit the liturgy is dead. But if a ritual is termed "sacramental," people are saying that it automatically confers inward grace on the participants. In the Roman Catholic church, when the priest prays over the bread and wine and says, *"Hoc est corpus meum"*—"This is my body"—it is believed that the bread and wine become the body and blood of Jesus. Therefore when you eat them, you are eating Jesus, and grace is conveyed to you, whether you feel it or not, whether you believe or not.

Though I accept the validity of a liturgical service, I do not accept that a rite or service can be sacramental. When we baptize someone, we do not believe that that person is being saved by the simple act of baptism.

There can be disadvantages in slavishly following a liturgy, and I touched on this in the chapter on tradition. It can mean that the service is superficial and mechanical. It can lead people to forget that they must depend on the Holy Spirit, and it can militate against expectancy and give a self-righteous feeling.

There are, I believe, three principles we should remember when we consider the place of liturgy in our church services. The first is that the aim of liturgy should be the glory of Christ. As Paul puts it in 2 Corinthians 3: "Nevertheless when anyone turns to the Lord, the veil is removed... But we all, seeing the glory of the Lord with unveiled faces, as in a mirror, are being transformed into the same image from glory to glory by the Spirit of the Lord" (vv. 16, 18).

The second principle is that the proof of a valid liturgy (as with a valid tradition, as we have seen) is that it gives freedom. Any liturgy that gives liberty is owned by the Spirit, for "where the Spirit of the Lord is, there is liberty" (2 Cor. 3:17). And liturgy that is of the Spirit will also produce growth and self-discipline. In 2 Corinthians Paul went on to say, "Therefore, since we have this ministry through the mercy we have received, we do not lose heart" (4:1).

The third principle is that many liturgies are temporary. In God's plan of redemption in the Bible we see a moving away from a set liturgy. In 2 Corinthians 3 Paul says that there are two kinds of worship. Both were given by God, both are called "glorious," and both had their proper place. One was by the Law, and the other is by the Spirit. Paul describes the former as "the ministration of condemnation" and the latter as "the ministration of righteousness" (2 Cor. 3:9). The law may have been glorious, but it had to be "done away" with (2 Cor. 3:11, KJV) and replaced by "a new and living way that He has opened for us" (Heb. 10:20). As Hebrews 8:13 puts it: "In speaking of a new covenant He has made the first one old. Now that which is decaying and growing old is ready to vanish away."

There are certain unchanging liturgies, but by and large liturgy is instituted for temporary situations, for the way God wants to be worshipped is by the impulse of the Spirit. We must have discernment to see what is changing and what is unchanging. The Lord's Prayer is an unchanging liturgy, and in the Bible there are timeless blessings that are liturgical in form, for example, Numbers 6:24–26: "The LORD bless you and keep you; the LORD make His face to shine upon you, and be gracious unto you; the LORD lift His countenance upon you, and give you peace." As we said, the Lord's Supper is an unchanging liturgy.

On the other hand, almost every liturgy that has come down through the history of the church has been temporary only. The second generation of any church, denomination, or movement must beware of keeping up a liturgy that is no longer relevant. Any liturgy that we have inherited should not be accepted uncritically. We must see whether its origin is in something unchanging from the Bible or whether it simply comes from a habit or mannerism or style that was born when the Spirit was present in power and no longer applies. For it is ridiculous to try to keep something up after the Spirit has gone.

We have got to be willing to follow what the Spirit is doing *today*. The impulse of the Spirit is our key, and it must take priority over any changeable liturgy. When Peter and John were on their way to the temple to pray and met the lame man, Peter stopped and healed him. Imagine John saying, "Hey, Peter, come on, we've got to be there by three o'clock. They're waiting for us!"

It takes not only spirituality, but courage, to see through an irrelevant liturgy. For we all have our comfortable liturgies. May God help us all to find the liturgy of the Spirit. It won't be written on a little prayer card. There will be no magical formulas to usher it in. It will be dictated by an inward peace that cannot be counterfeited. When the Spirit resides ungrieved in the hearts of a congregation, something will happen that defies a natural explanation, and everyone will know that the new has come. When the Spirit is present, the only thing to do is to step aside and let Him have His way. And then there will be liberty and great glory.

CHAPTER 23

THE JOY OF DOING NOTHING

*In returning and rest you shall be saved; in quietness
and in confidence shall be your strength.*

—Isaiah 30:15

S O FAR WE have been thinking a great deal about what we can *do* in worship—admittedly in response to the Holy Spirit—but nevertheless our actions of praying, praising, listening, loving, and obeying. And of course there is nothing wrong with that. But there is a much deeper level of worship, one in which we are unable to express ourselves verbally or non-verbally—where we are utterly passive. The highest and most intense worship takes place when we can do nothing but be amazed, when we are rendered helpless and speechless with wonder and gratitude, when we just sit back and watch God work. This is what Isaiah is talking about when he says, "For thus says the Lord GOD, the Holy One of Israel: In returning and rest you shall be saved; in quietness and in confidence shall be your strength" (Isa. 30:15).

In worship at this depth we are kept from even saying, "Thank You." For, at the risk of being misunderstood, I am prepared to say that our gratitude sometimes gets in the way of praise. Gratitude can be an attempt to get the balance even again. Probably you have experienced on a human level something of what I am getting at. Someone does something for you, and you know very well that he or she wants you to be thankful, and you are, so you express your gratitude. You try to be extremely thankful so that this person will really see how you feel. Or you try to return the favor in some way. This gives you a feeling of satisfaction.

Have you ever been placed in a situation in which there was nothing you could say or do? Someone did something immensely wonderful, and you weren't able to do anything but feel grateful? Perhaps the person went away, and you wished you could find him or her to say how much you appreciated what was done. And maybe you felt frustrated, and some of your joy was taken away because it was not possible to express your gratitude. On the natural level we always feel that we must do something.

But Isaiah says that our salvation lies in the fact that we do nothing: "In returning and rest you shall be saved." I did not say that we feel nothing, but that we do nothing. This, says Isaiah, is the best way to live—the way God wants us to live. It constitutes the greatest joy there is. And even though we are rendered helpless—as though we are just standing there with our mouth wide open—God sees how we feel and knows that we are grateful.

Yet, though this is what God wanted, the people Isaiah was speaking to would not do this. It reads: "...in quietness and in confidence shall be your strength. *Yet you were not willing*" (Isa. 30:15, emphasis added). The people wanted to "do" instead. They said, "No, for we will flee on horses ...We will ride on swift horses" (v. 16). And that's the way so many of us are. We can't imagine getting satisfaction from anything but "doing." We must be always working, always on the go. We feel guilty if we are not on the move.

Isaiah 30:15 is set in the context of a solemn rebuke. The people of Israel thought that they had better ideas than God on how to fight their battles—and they had actually turned to Egypt for help. The chapter begins, "Woe to the rebellious children, says the LORD, who take counsel, but not from Me...they walk down to Egypt and have not asked from My mouth, to strengthen themselves in the safety of Pharaoh and to trust in the shadow of Egypt!" (vv. 1–2). They thought that God would understand if they turned to the resources of Egypt for help to fight His battles. They wouldn't listen when God said, "This is a rebellious people, lying children, children who refuse to listen to the law of the LORD" (v. 9). They only wanted to hear pleasant things. Verse 10 says, "They say to the seers, 'You must not see visions,' and to the prophets, 'You must not prophesy to us right things; speak to us pleasant things, prophesy illusions.'" As a result, although they claimed that they were doing the Lord's work, they were really rejecting the Holy One of Israel.

And the Lord said to them, "Therefore this iniquity shall be to you as a breach ready to fall, swelling up in a high wall, whose collapse comes suddenly, in an instant" (v. 13). They would be destroyed as completely as pottery breaks in pieces: "[God] shall break it as the breaking of the potter's vessel that is broken in pieces; He shall not spare so that there shall not be found in the breaking of it a shard to take fire from the hearth" (v. 14).

And it is at this point that Isaiah had the boldness to tell the people what God envisaged for them: "For thus says the Lord GOD, the Holy One of Israel: In returning and rest you shall be saved" (v. 15). Not in going to Egypt, but in just looking to God and relying on him. "In quietness and in confidence shall be your strength" (v. 15). All God asked for was the complete trust of the people. He wanted them to get their joy from seeing Him accomplish His Word. But they wouldn't have it.

Two Christian doctrines emerge here, the first of which is justification—being made righteous in God's sight—by faith alone. Romans 4:2 says, "If Abraham was justified by works, he has something to boast about, but not before God." And verse 5 says, "But to him who does not work, but believes in Him who justifies the ungodly, his faith is credited as righteousness." So if any of us think we will go to heaven when we die because we've tried to live a good life and haven't done much wrong and haven't hurt anybody, then we must see that we are wrong and are at this moment on the way to hell. God does not justify us because of our actions or our words. Justification comes simply by trusting in what Jesus did on the cross.

The second doctrine concerns the living of the Christian life. Our Christian life must be lived without confidence in works. I don't mean it's to be lived without works, but it is to be lived without relying on what we do to get God's approval. We must not feel conscious of any good we are doing but must consider that what we are doing is nothing. Jesus said, "But when you do your charitable deeds, do not let your left hand know what your right hand is doing" (Matt. 6:3). And Paul says in Galatians 2:20: "I have been crucified with Christ. It is no longer I who live, but Christ who lives in me. And the life I now live in the flesh, I live by faith in the Son of God, who loved me and gave Himself for me." As long as we are conscious of our works or derive our assurance from them—as long we are so impertinent as to conclude that we are saved because we do good things—then we grieve the Spirit and cut ourselves off from the joy that can be ours just by trusting in His Word alone.

If we are living in frustration and bondage, always checking our spiritual pulse to see whether or not God loves us and whether we are saved, we show that we are only looking to ourselves. As Calvin said, "If you contemplate yourself, that is sure damnation."[1] It is idolatry, for it shows we are not looking to God.

God just wants us to believe His Word. And His Word says that, if we look to Him, we are saved. "There is life in a look," said Spurgeon.[2] "In quietness and in confidence shall be your strength" (Isa. 30:15).

When we are in heaven singing the praises of God, we will know that God did it all from start to finish. But Isaiah's point is: See this now. Live like this now. Because that is where our strength in living lies. When some people get to heaven and finally realize that they were saved by grace alone, they will look back and think of all the guilt and frustration they went through here below, all their anxiety and rushing about, all their questioning, "Am I a Christian?", and will see just how useless it all was.

After years and years of the Christian life many people still worry about whether they are really Christians. But this is of the devil. He tries to paralyze us and keep us looking inward for our confidence. Whereas if we settled it once and for all by trusting God's Word, we could get on with our life and with worshipping God.

Isaiah is saying, "Don't wait until you get to heaven to find out that you were saved all along! See it now and it will change your whole lifestyle. You will see God work in a manner that you never dreamed of!"

I fear also that so much of our worship today is motivated by self-righteousness. We sing our hymns, pray pious prayers, and tell God how much we love Him. Then we leave the church feeling really good inside—but it makes God sick. We are like the person who talks about himself all the time; he may enjoy it, but everybody else is thoroughly fed up!

Remember that Simon Peter, after he had walked with the Lord for three years, said, "I will lay down my life for Your sake." Yet Jesus said to him, "Will you lay down your life for My sake? Truly, truly I say to you, the rooster shall not crow until you have denied Me three times" (John 13:37–38).

We may get a good feeling out of saying, "Lord, I love You." But He sees right through us.

Yet the marvel is that Jesus kept right on speaking to Peter. As I have already said, in the Greek there were no commas or full stops, much less chapters and verses. This means that Jesus actually said to Peter, "The rooster shall not crow until you have denied Me three times. Let not your heart be troubled. You believe in God. Believe also in Me" (John 13:38–14:1). Here is one who knew what Peter was going to do, yet He said, "Let not your heart be troubled. You believe in God. Believe also in Me."

We are saved through His grace—not by whether we keep our word of promise to Him.

So much of our worship is aimed at getting a good feeling for ourselves. We think we have shown God how much we love Him, or we feel we have paid our dues, as it were, or have gained some leverage with God by going to church. But God spoke as He did in Isaiah 30:15 because He wanted the people of Israel to see His total grace and their total helplessness. He wanted them to see His power alone.

Do you know the feeling of having fallen and having been forgiven? If you haven't, then there is a sense in which you are impoverished. I suppose one of the most controversial things Martin Luther ever said was his advice to Melanchthon: "Sin lustily, that grace may abound." Taken out of context, such a statement is dangerous and can easily be misunderstood. But Melanchthon was a very delicate, self-righteous person who wouldn't dream of doing anything wrong in a thousand years. And he wasn't really enjoying the grace of God. Luther meant that if he were to fall real good, when he came to God, he would feel forgiven and fresh.

But we certainly don't need to fall in an obviously bad way for that to happen. Sometimes God will just let us see what is there in our hearts—that inability to forgive, that need to vindicate ourselves, all that wickedness. And when we see that God accepts us with all that, it is marvelous. Self-righteous people can never truly worship, for they have no sense of sin.

Isaiah very much wanted the people to enjoy hearing the voice of God. The way to do this is through *rest*! "In returning and rest you shall be saved." Hebrews 4:10 says, "For whoever enters His rest will also cease from his own works, as God did from His." And the key phrase here is, "from his own works." We need to stop feeling the need to be always on the go. We must stop getting our joy from "being involved." If we are frustrated and burnt out, then there is no trust. But when we cease from our work and just do nothing—then we see that God likes us just the way we are—and that is when we worship!

Do we think that we are only important to God when we are doing something? Isaiah says, "In returning and rest you shall be saved; in quietness and in confidence shall be your strength" (30:15). This is the way God wants us to live. When someone does something wonderful for us, we may not always be able to thank them, and they'll never know how we feel. But with God we can be left in awe, and He does know how we feel. He just wants us to enjoy seeing Him do what He by Himself alone can do.

This is far more than the first ABC of holy living. Some people are paralyzed because they have never got beyond the first steps in sanctification. The first steps are important, but we must move beyond that level. What Isaiah is doing here—and what the Holy Spirit is doing today—is giving each of us an invitation to enter the big league.

"By faith Noah, being divinely warned about things not yet seen, moved with godly fear, prepared an ark to save his family" (Heb. 11:7). Noah saw God do marvelous things. Abraham trusted God and got Isaac back. Jacob was a man who had seen sorrow, for he had lost Joseph. He had been a scoundrel from the word *go*, but he got Joseph back, and at the end of his days he could be found leaning on his staff and saying, "God is so good." He knew he didn't deserve anything. He just worshipped. By faith Joseph saw that his bones would be taken back to Canaan when the nation returned. Moses saw the children of Israel cross the Red Sea on dry land; all he could do was stand in amazement and watch. Joshua in his turn saw the walls of Jericho fall.

And that's how God wants it to be with us. He wants us to trust and see Him work.

But as long as we are always on the go, trying to bring in the kingdom by our activism, God will just fold His hands and say, "You want to do it? Go on then." There was a time when Abraham got impatient and ran ahead of God. He had no children, and Sarah was old, yet God had told him that he would have a son. When the child did not come, he lay with Hagar, Sarah's servant girl. And for fourteen years Abraham thought Ishmael was his promised heir.

Then one day God said, "Sarah will conceive." And she did, and Isaac was born.

How many of us today have wanted to see God act, and so have fallen into this same mistake of rushing in and making something happen and then calling it the work of God?

Isaiah 30:18 says, "Therefore, the LORD longs to be gracious to you, and therefore, He waits on high to have mercy on you; for the LORD is a God of justice; how blessed are all who long for Him."

Have you wondered why God isn't working? It's because you're doing the work. So God says, "I'll just wait." And when we run ahead rather than rest, we will always be sorry. When the Israelites said, "We will flee on horses...We will ride on swift horses" (Isa. 30:16), God said in effect, "You certainly will run. You'll stay on the run, and your pursuers will be swift. The day will come when you will have to look to Me, and I will be gracious then to you."

Some people are anxious to vindicate themselves—to clear their name from some lie. They meddle here and pull a string there. And God says, "Oh, you want to do it? Go on, then. I'll just wait." And they make a bigger and bigger mess of things. Others are trying to fight their own battles or to nudge the arm of God's providence. Well, God said, "You try that, and you'll be more vulnerable than ever." Verse 17 says they would be "left as a flag on the top of a mountain and as a banner on a hill." They would be a wide open target for all to see their folly.

Many people can't imagine that doing it God's way—the way of faith alone—could turn things around. Some people are running their business affairs in a way that is dishonoring to God, and they say, "Well, we live in a wicked world. We just have to do some of these little shady things." They're frustrated and in trouble because God has folded His arms and said, "Go on—you try it your way." But if they would get it right with God, He'd bless them. He may not make them millionaires, but they'll have peace—which is something they don't have now.

Some people, though they are Christians, are looking to the

world for happiness. They think that by living with that worldly crowd, or by going to one more movie or one more bar, they will somehow get satisfaction. And they justify themselves by saying, "God understands that I have needs." And God lets them do it—but they don't have peace.

There are two principles here that, if we can grasp them, will result in the kind of worship God seeks of us. The first, as we have seen from Isaiah 30:15 and Hebrews 4:10, is that of operating without any fatigue. This is what happens when we get right with God. We just come to Him and do it His way. As the NIV puts it, "In repentance and rest is your salvation." *Repentance* means "change of mind." It means saying, "God got it right. I agree with Him."

How many people are utterly frustrated? They have tried everything and the result has only been fatigue. I was talking recently to a minister who said to me, "I've had to ask for a sabbatical. I'm burnt out."

When we don't wait on God and are always trying to do things ourselves, the result is endless turmoil. But if we really want assurance of salvation, God will knock everything out from under us until we trust Him alone.

To rest in God means that we leave everything to Him. We leave it to Him to put us in the right place at the right time, and with the right people at the right time, even in the right financial position at the right time. And why is this the way of no fatigue? Well, it is because we get our approval from the blood of Christ and not from our works, and because we live by the authority of the Spirit of Christ.

The result is that we live and worship in a state of amazement, awe, and admiration, which is the second principle I want us to see from Isaiah 30:15. This is because we believe the promise of 1 John 1:9: "If we confess our sins, He is faithful and just to forgive us our sins and cleanse us from all unrighteousness." The blood of Jesus washes away our sin as though it had never been committed, and a fresh beginning always follows. The result is quietness, peace, and ease.

And we have quietness over the most difficult situations, quietness over our deepest fears. For God says, "Leave it to Me." We lose the desire to get even with those who have hurt us, and we feel little need to prove ourselves. Brother Lawrence says that he could get his joy from leaning over and picking up a piece of straw from the ground.[3] That is what Isaiah 30:15 is talking about.

Real worship is directed towards One who doesn't want anything from us for what He has done for us. There are no strings attached. God only wants us to trust Him. He wants us to experience the joy of doing nothing, nothing but resting on the fact that He loves us. God wants us just to look to Him and say, "Lord, I don't know how much I love You. But I know how much You love me." Rest on that and let God love you. Then you will stand in awe.

Then to our surprise we begin to hear God's voice giving us clear instructions. As verse 21 of Isaiah 30 puts it: "Your ears shall hear a word behind you, saying, 'This is the way, walk in it.'" Note the order: first we rest on the fact that God loves us and then we hear Him speak.

It is a way of no fatigue and of continual amazement.

Mr. Poole-Connor, the man who founded the Fellowship of Independent Evangelical Churches, lived into his nineties, and before he died, he said, "The longer I live and the older I get, the more amazed I am that God sent His Son into the world to die on a cross for my sins."

That's the way we are saved. That's the way we are to live. And that's what will bring true worship by the Holy Spirit.

CHAPTER 24

WORSHIP AND REVIVAL

*At midnight Paul and Silas were praying and singing
hymns to God, and the prisoners were listening to them.*

—ACTS 16:25

R EVIVAL IS THE sovereign intervention of God—and it
is for this that we are all longing and waiting. When
revival comes, there will be no more need for books on
worship!

But what can we do till then? Do we just wait? Is it point-
less to think about worship when we know revival will clarify it
and straighten it out? Well, we can do something. As Donald
Grey Barnhouse used to say: "While we wait, we can worship."

When Paul came to Philippi, revival came upon the people
there who were seeking God. It started with Lydia, a seller of
purple fabric. Luke says that Lydia "heard us. The Lord opened
her heart to acknowledge what Paul said" (Acts 16:14). Three
types of worship can be seen here. We could call them traditional worship, transitional worship, and transformed worship.

Before Paul arrived, Lydia worshipped God in the traditional way, as she had been taught. She did worship God—but
something needed to happen to her. She needed new life. I
think this is the way it is with many churches.

When Lydia listened to Paul, her worship entered a transitional stage. And I think even more churches are in this stage.
Christians in this country are listening, praying, and waiting.
We are all longing for transformed worship, which comes when,
as with Lydia, the Lord opens our hearts.

In Lydia we see revival in miniature. But she was part of a wider movement of the Spirit. It is helpful for us to see what happened when Paul came to Philippi and how he saw revival there.

The worship and revival described in Acts 16 began with an unexpected change of plan. We read in verse 6 that they "were forbidden by the Holy Spirit to speak the word in Asia." Whereupon Paul and his companions came to Mysia. They wanted to go to Bithynia, but again the Spirit wouldn't let them. They must have felt very confused, for they had never known anything like this before. There was nothing wrong with what they were wanting to do. No one could argue that their desire to preach the gospel in Asia was wrong. That is true of so much that is traditional: you can't call it wrong exactly.

All this may have been unsettling and even scary for Paul and Silas. And that is how many of us feel about the whole subject of revival and why many don't want revival and hold back on it. People like to have things planned. The unplanned and spontaneous is disturbing and alarming.

It has been said that a great work of the Spirit often begins with confusion, and that to confuse is the first work of the Holy Spirit. Perhaps that is happening to you as you read this book, and you wonder what is going on. Well, it may be that God is up to something great. What should you do? Paul and Silas let God lead them. They obeyed the Spirit. And following upon their obedience there came a vision. We read in verse 9: "During the night a vision appeared to Paul: A man of Macedonia stood and pleaded with him, saying, 'Come over to Macedonia and help us.'"

There is no virtue in change for the sake of change. The proof that change is right is that there is fresh vision. I know of churches that have gotten bored with the way they have been doing things and introduced changes. But because they lacked a vision from God, they have been worse off as a result of their changes. But how do we know that the vision is of God? Following Paul's obedience to the vision, there were conversions, beginning with Lydia. Any vision and change that doesn't lead to conversions has got to be held suspect.

Some years ago a very close friend of mine, Bruce Porter, pastor of a church down in the Florida Keys, asked me for advice about proposed changes in his church. I said, "The proof that you're led of the Spirit is that there will be conversions like you've never had before. That will be the test. If you don't have them, back off. If you have them, God is with you, because only God can save. A conversion is a seal of God."

The result for my friend was that they had more conversions than they had ever had, and today I believe church attendance has doubled.

This movement of God, which began with unexpected change and led on to conversions, was marked by friendship. The word *comrade* is used among Marxists and Communists, but they haven't a clue about true comradeship. To find that, we need to look in the New Testament.

Here in Acts 16:15 we read that when Lydia was baptized, "she entreated us, saying, 'If you have judged me to be faithful to the Lord, come to my house and remain there.'" This was spontaneous friendship, and it is one of the characteristics of revival. There is nothing forced or false about the fellowship that comes when the Spirit is present. When the Spirit is moving, hearts are knit together and a new fellowship emerges between people who thought they had nothing in common and no natural affinity.

But here in Philippi the worship was paralleled by undesirable competition. In verses 16 and 17 we read, "On one occasion, as we went to the place of prayer, a servant girl possessed with a spirit of divination [an ability to forecast the future] met us, who brought her masters much profit by fortune-telling. She followed Paul and us, shouting, 'These men are servants of the Most High God, who proclaim to us the way of salvation.'"

What do we do about this sort of undesirable competition? Strange as it may seem, we ought to look at odd people suddenly coming on the scene as a not unhealthy sign, uncomfortable though it makes us feel, because revival has a way of attracting people like this.

Two illustrations will bear out the point I want to make. One you may think is a ridiculous illustration, but it has served as a great lesson for me. I've already written about Bonefish Sam, who is a bonefish guide in Bimini. He is a legend in the Bahamas. All the tourist literature back in the fifties would feature Bonefish Sam, who was then only in his thirties. He was featured years ago in *Life* magazine. I used to go out with Bonefish Sam, but he has now gone to heaven.

Sam told this interesting story about how there was one spot where you could always find a lot of bonefish. The trouble was, you couldn't catch them there because little mangrove shoots grew around, and whenever you cast your line, should a fish take the bait, it would catch on the mangrove shoots and break the line. It was so exasperating. One day Bonefish Sam had an idea. He went out and pulled up all those mangrove shoots. There must have been dozens and dozens of them. He cleared the whole area out so that when he went back there again, we would be able to catch a lot of fish. But when he went back, there were no fish at all. They didn't return until the mangrove shoots grew back. Trying to weed them out killed the whole thing. That's the first illustration.

The second one is a famous story about Whitefield and Wesley. When Whitefield went to the fields and preached, God came down on him and those around him in power and great things happened. People would shout, they would bark like dogs, they would jerk. Fanaticism, no doubt, was a part of it, and John Wesley, a dignified Anglican, criticized Whitefield for allowing that. He told him to weed it out and remove what was false. Whitefield wisely replied that if you try to remove what you don't like, you will destroy the real as well. He said that you just have to let it go and leave it to God to deal with.

Here is a verse that I cling to: "[Jesus] answered, 'Every plant which My heavenly Father has not planted will be uprooted'" (Matt 15:13). However, God knows how much we can bear. The girl who was calling out after Paul disturbed him for many days. That shows how patient Paul was. But there came a time when he said, "Enough is enough," and he dealt with it. God will show us when we must deal with the sort of thing that militates against His purposes and the working of His Spirit. But we must be careful that when we act it is truly from the Spirit.

The worship was also accompanied by controversy. This happened because Paul cast the devil out of this woman. We read, "When her masters saw that the hope of their profits was gone, they seized Paul and Silas, and dragged them into the marketplace to the rulers. And they brought them to the magistrates, saying, 'These men, being Jews, greatly trouble our city and teach customs which are not lawful for us, being Romans, to receive or observe'" (Acts 16:19–21).

Internal difficulties led to external controversy. Paul had dealt with the problem that threatened their worship, and Satan was very angry. As a result the world outside was now affected. We don't have to worry too much about how to reach the world outside when we are faithful to what is going on internally.

We wish everybody would rejoice when revival comes, but they won't because revival exposes sin. Revival breathes holiness, and men don't like holiness. The world doesn't want it. People in the world don't see that sin in the heart must be dealt with before there can be real social changes. One of the curses of the modern church is that it has become enamored with the social gospel and has sometimes become preoccupied with lobbying and trying to get laws passed in Congress. Social change can take place only when the heart is dealt with.

When Paul healed the demon-possessed girl, it hurt the pockets of those who had hired her. I believe that Paul's words, "The love of money is the root of all evil" (1 Tim. 6:10) are to be taken literally. The devil is stirred up when a person's wallet is touched. It is then you have a fight on your hands. Voltaire, the French atheist who got his greatest pleasure from criticizing Christianity, used to say that when it comes to money, every man's religion is the same.[1] We need to think very carefully whether the love of money has a grip on us. You may think, "That's no problem with me. I don't have any money!" But you may be surprised at how much you cling to the little you don't have!

The overreaction of these men resulted in false accusations: "These men...teach customs which are not lawful for us, being Romans, to receive or observe'" (Acts 16:21). That was simply not true. Paul's accusers didn't say what the real problem was. When Satan is at work, lies spread rapidly and those not on the side of truth believe them. The result was that Paul and Silas were put in jail.

What then? Do you think Silas looked over to Paul and said, "What have we done? We can't be in God's will; we're in prison. Maybe we were wrong. We felt that we weren't supposed to go into Bithynia or Asia, but maybe we should have gone, Paul"?

Do you think Paul replied, "I know. We're in prison. We couldn't have been in God's will. When you are in God's will, you never have problems. What are we going to do?"

What really happened? In Acts 16:25 we read, "At midnight Paul and Silas were praying and singing hymns to God, and the prisoners were listening to them." They continued to worship with undaunted courage.

When revival comes, you just can't stop people worshipping God. When people are filled with the Holy Spirit, the time and the place don't matter. The hallmark of real, fervent worship is spontaneity.

One of the stories that often comes out about true revival is that people don't need as much sleep as they usually need. In the Welsh Revival they would go to church and stay there till the early hours of the morning and get up and go to work and not feel tired.

But more was to come for Paul and Silas. The next thing we see was an unusual coincidence: "Suddenly there was a great earthquake, so that the foundations of the prison were shaken. And immediately all the doors were opened and everyone's shackles were loosened" (Acts 16:26). An earthquake just happened to come along at that moment while they were singing praises to God. This coincidence of the earthquake and Paul and Silas worshipping was a seal of the sovereign, glorified God. It is often the case when revival is at its height that extraordinary things happen that defy a natural explanation.

A lot of people say, "When I see that happen, I'll believe revival is coming." But when it comes to that stage, those who are still waiting to decide whether it is really a work of God are detached from it to such a degree that they don't get any pleasure from it. There can be a deep weeping and wailing and gnashing of teeth when people see God at work and are left out because at the beginning they held back. "He who is faithful in what is least is faithful also in much. And he who is dishonest in the least is dishonest also in much" (Luke 16:10).

More happened: unexpected conversions. We read that the keeper of the prison woke up and, when he saw the prison doors open, he drew out his sword to kill himself. He knew he would be held responsible for the prisoners' escape and would be killed in their place. But Paul said, "Don't be afraid. We're here. Don't hurt yourself." (See Acts 16:28.)

Then the jailer asked an interesting question: "What must I do to be saved?" (Acts 16:29). This shows that Paul and Silas must have been witnessing to him. How else would a jailer know about being saved? It's not exactly the sort of language you would expect to hear in jail. Nor is it language that is much in vogue today. I was talking to a minister recently who said he likes to use the word *committed*; *saved* was a bit too holy or too old-fashioned for him—or for many people.

The jailer and all his family became believers that night. Isn't it wonderful that God should use an earthquake to get to one family? God can do it, for He wants to save His own, and He will go to extraordinary means to bring about response.

In this revival in Philippi there was preaching, singing, witnessing, conversions, and a touch of the extraordinary. There was competition, controversy, confrontations. Then, finally, there was undoubted clarification. What had begun with change and confusion ended with joy. Looking back, Paul and Silas could see the hand of God in it all.

How is it with us? God puts tests before us. Do we have a clear vision for the lost? Will we panic when we see undesirable competition? Are we afraid of controversy?

I have already mentioned the summer of 1956. It was a very dark time for me. Some months before I had experienced entering into God's rest, and I thought that my family would all be thrilled to bits when they heard of what God was doing in me. I had discovered truths that only God could have shown to me, but my family wasn't so happy. A year or so before, my grandmother, so proud of her grandson, the first minister in the family, had bought me a brand new 1955 Chevrolet, a beautiful car, but when I began to displease her, she took it back. One relative called me a shame and a disgrace to the family. My friends distanced themselves from me.

One Sunday afternoon I remember listening to "The Old-Fashioned Revival Hour," a radio program with Charles E. Fuller. I was reminded that God knows the way through wilderness, and all we need to do is follow Him.

If we do this, He will show us what He is up to in our lives and in our churches.

CHAPTER 25

PREPARATION FOR ULTIMATE WORSHIP

*...and after the fire, a still, small voice. When
Elijah heard it, he wrapped his face in his cloak.*

—1 Kings 19:12–13

THIS BOOK HAS been based on a series of sermons I gave at Westminster Chapel. One evening as I walked home towards the end of the series, one of the deacons asked me what I thought I had learned from my messages on worship. In reply I said that not only had I learned that any worthwhile worship is done by the Spirit of God, but that I had come to understand how important worship actually is.

If only every Christian would become more gripped by a sense of the importance of worship, it would make a great difference to our church life and witness. I wonder whether we realize that God not only cares about the kind of worship we give, but also really wants our worship. I find it so moving that God should care about my worship of Him.

Our natural reaction to this idea is to think, "Well, worship of God by little old me isn't going to matter to Him!" We tend to think that God will take more notice of the worship of more important people, like the Queen of England, or the US President, or an eminent man of God such as Billy Graham. When God sees these people at worship, we feel He must say, "Ah, this is more like it!" Maybe we don't say this in so many words, but isn't it what we so often secretly feel?

Yet running right through the Bible is the theme that God

cares about each individual as though there were no one else to care for. Whether you are five years old, or fifty, or ninety, God cares about your worship. He is not interested in your status in life; He looks at you.

On Palm Sunday when the children were crying, "Hosanna to the son of David," the chief priests and scribes didn't like it. But Jesus said to them, "Have you never read, 'Out of the mouth of children and infants You have perfected praise'?" (Matt. 21:15–16).

There are not any people alive now who were present at the Welsh Revival. But many years ago I used to spend time with Mrs. Martyn Lloyd-Jones. She was there in Wales when she was a child of six. She lived in London, but when her father heard that revival had broken out in Wales, he took her out of school and sent her there. He argued that she could always go to school, but she might never see revival again.

Mrs. Lloyd-Jones told me that at the peak of the revival, her older brother, who was eight, stood up in the service and began to pray. She said his face shone like an angel, and he prayed on and on until finally their grandfather went up to him and said, "All right, you can sit down now." Such was the worship of a child.

You see, not only do so-called unimportant people matter, but God does not care whether or not you are in a strategic position from which to help spread His name. You may sometimes think, "I'm not going to be able to do anything for God where I am. Why should He show me anything or give me any insights? But I think I can prove to you that God wants our worship irrespective of our "usefulness."

The proof I can offer is the example of Elijah. "Well, yes," you may say, "of course, God would want to show Elijah something. But I'm not Elijah. Why would God talk to me?"

But what God had to show Elijah came at a time when his work was virtually over and he had nothing more left to do for God. Elderly people, who are now housebound, can recall days when they were of use in the world. Now they feel useless.

Other people feel that they have no gift and are utterly insignificant. Why should God waste His time revealing Himself to them when there is no way they can pass the revelation on to help other people? Yet here was Elijah, getting his most profound insight into the nature of God when he had nothing more to do in the world.

First Kings 19:9 says of him, "He came to a cave and camped there, and the word of the LORD came to him, and He said to him, 'Why are you here, Elijah?'" The text continues:

> And he said, "I have been very zealous for the LORD, Lord of Hosts, for the children of Israel have forsaken Your covenant, thrown down Your altars, and killed Your prophets with the sword, and I alone am left, and they seek to take my life." He said, "Go and stand on the mountain before the LORD." And, behold, the LORD passed by, and a great and strong wind split the mountains and broke in pieces the rocks before the LORD, but the LORD was not in the wind. And after the wind, an earthquake came, but the LORD was not in the earthquake. And after the earthquake, a fire came, but the LORD was not in the fire.
>
> —1 KINGS 10:10–12

Then come these remarkable words: "And after the fire, a still, small voice. When Elijah heard it, he wrapped his face in his cloak" (vv. 12–13).

Elijah worshipped God. What matters to God is not how important we are or how useful we are. All that matters to Him is the quality of our worship. We may ask, "Why did God not reveal Himself in the stillness earlier on?" Could Elijah not have been more useful to God over the years if he had known about true worship when he was young? Why did he only discover what he did about God and himself right at the end of his life?

The answer is that God was preparing Elijah to worship

Him and to do nothing else. The only thing that was left for Elijah to do was to give his mantle to Elisha and anoint Jehu as king (1 Kings 19:15–16). This shows us that there is knowledge of God that a man uses for worship and nothing else. In humanistic education it is said that the only knowledge that is worthwhile is utilitarian knowledge. But God showed Elijah something very profound that he never used.

Worship that is pleasing to God has several characteristics, the first of which is insight: the awareness of God that precipitates and inspires the worship. Next there is integrity: the ability of the worshipper to come before God in truth, with his whole self, and no little corners held back. Then there is indebtedness: the sense of our debt to God. As Isaac Watts put it:

> Here, Lord, I give myself away,
> 'Tis all that I can do.[1]

Fourth, there is a sense of inadequacy: our inability to express the depth of our feelings towards God. Charles Wesley could only say:

> O for a thousand tongues to sing
> My great Redeemer's praise.[2]

And this quality of worship is possible only through the Holy Spirit. You cannot worship beyond the level of your insight. The intensity of your worship reflects the depth of your insight. And you get that insight by the Holy Spirit. A feeling of indebtedness is proof that you realize that your insight is from God. A sense of inadequacy will also determine the quantity or length of time of your worship. You feel you must keep on trying to express your love and need of God. And this will continue throughout eternity. For we will always be unable to express our debt to God because we are in heaven and not hell.

True worship exposes our imperfection. It matters to God

that we should see how imperfect we are. One of the most painful, as well as usually one of the last, things we discover about ourselves is that we are self-righteous. Elijah was self-righteous. He said to God, "I have been very zealous for the LORD, Lord of hosts...and I alone am left" (1 Kings 19:10). And even after he had heard the "still, small voice," this imperfection was still there. In verse 14 he is saying exactly the same thing: "I have been very zealous for the LORD, Lord of hosts...and I alone am left."

And God had used this self-righteous man. Elijah was a most extraordinary man, one who could go to a king and say, "It's not going to rain again for three years—not until I say it will." It was Elijah who challenged and confronted the prophets of Baal on Mount Carmel in one of the highest moments in the history of world redemption.

It can be a great comfort to us that, as James said, Elijah was "a man subject to like passions as we are" (James 5:17). God can use us as we are, with all our inadequacies and lack of understanding. We always think we have to be so well-equipped, so full of knowledge, before God can use us in His work here on earth. And that is not true. Heaven will reveal insight after insight about God: knowledge of God for His own sake. And we think, "If only I had known this before, I could have been more useful to God.

But God does not necessarily show us things so that we can use them or teach them to others. He does not need men who have great knowledge or strategic people who have insight. He does not get His pleasure out of great numbers of people knowing this or that. Instead He loves to reveal the profoundest truth to one person who may be absolutely unknown—or who may never tell it to anyone, much less use it.

It is very important to know this because it shows us that our greatest joy and pleasure is to be found in God alone. So much of what is pleasurable in this life has to be shared with somebody else in order to be fully enjoyed. Even if we had tea with the Queen, much of the joy would be in sharing what we had experienced. But the joy of being in the presence of God alone is the greatest joy there is, and it does not need to be shared.

Suppose you have accomplished every goal you ever wanted to achieve. You have met everyone you wanted to meet, gone everywhere you wanted to go. What's left?

Elijah was like this. He could not have wanted to achieve more. He had been in the presence of the king, he had travelled both inside and outside Israel, and above all, he had lived to see the prophets of Baal destroyed. What was there left for him?

What was left was the inexhaustible God. David put it like this in Psalm 16:11: "In Your presence is fullness of joy; at Your right hand there are pleasures for evermore." The greatest joy there is lies in God. It's not sex. It's not money. It's not drink or travel or a nice car and good home or the love of our family or learning or music. Whatever your age, the greatest joy there is, is to be found in God.

Many young people say, "Heaven sounds rather boring to me if all we are going to do there is worship God." But they say this because they have not yet had a taste of His presence. They are living so much at the natural level that they can conceive nothing else. But, as I hope to show in the next chapter, heaven will be an eternal, never-ending, ever-increasing insight into the glory and power, the wisdom and holiness of God. Every day in eternity with Jesus will be sweeter than the one before.

And so, after he had seen God work in such a powerful manner all his life, Elijah was given a profound insight. He realized that he had a lot more to learn about God. He had discovered that there were still seven thousand true worshippers in Israel. He saw that God had used him even though he hadn't known these things. And he realized that he hadn't needed to know them in order to be of use to God. Finally, he learned that some knowledge of God does not have to be shared with others.

The greatest thing that we can do here below is to worship by God's Spirit. Maybe we will even see that all we do here is but a rehearsal for our worship in heaven. And God may show us something that is just for us, tempted though we may be to tell it to others. Because God cares that we should worship Him with a sense of intensity and indebtedness, of inadequacy yet of almost uncontainable joy. That's what God wants. He doesn't need millions. But He wants you and me.

CHAPTER 26

WORSHIP IN HEAVEN

Look! I am making all things new.

—Revelation 21:5

I FINISHED THE LAST chapter by saying that what matters to God is my worship of Him. And my worship and knowledge of God is not a means to an end, but an end in itself. For that is the way I will spend eternity: worshipping God for God's own sake, and knowing that this brings Him pleasure. That is what will make heaven, heaven.

Isn't this exciting? We are going to heaven. A man said to me, "I'm looking forward to worship in heaven." Sometimes I can hardly wait.

But what about our worship in heaven? Will we still be worshipping by the Spirit?

The answer is, "Yes." This is because in heaven we will have the Spirit without measure. That is the way it was with Jesus here on earth (John 3:34). When we get to heaven, we shall see Jesus as He is, and we shall be like Him. So in heaven we will worship perfectly by the Spirit.

And what about preaching—for we have said that worship is the preparation for and response to the preached Word? I don't suppose there will be any preaching in heaven, but throughout all eternity our worship will be the response to the preached Word, for it is because of the preached Word that we first came to trust Jesus and to be saved. As Paul says, "It pleased God through the foolishness of preaching to save those who believe" (1 Cor. 1:21).

If we want to understand something about the nature of worship, we must look at John's vision of heaven in Revelation, for there we get a glimpse of true and pure praise and adoration of God. We have already seen something of this: of the singing and joy, the praising and music in heaven. This is not poetic exaggeration. "Write," said the angel to John, "for these words are faithful and true" (Rev. 21:5).

In Revelation 21:5 we read: "Look! I am making all things new." That means there will be things that are different about our worship in heaven.

What won't we be doing in heaven? First, there will be no soul-winning in heaven. That is one enterprise that will be finished forever (though for some Christians it's never started!). I speculate that the angels will remember nostalgically those old concerts and choirs when they sang over sinners that repented. It won't be happening in heaven. All the people that ever lived, however many, billions and billions, will all be forever in heaven or in hell. There will be no further population growth. There will be no tithing, no intercessory prayer, no warnings.

Second, there will be no sin in heaven. John said, "No unclean thing shall ever enter it" (Rev. 21:27). Through the blood of Christ we are saved, first from the penalty of sin, second from the power of sin, but third—and this part is in the future—from the presence of sin. When that day comes, we will have perfect bodies. There will be no sin in body, mind, soul, or spirit.

There will be no scoffing in heaven. John tells us that "the cowardly, the unbelieving, the abominable, the murderers, the sexually immoral, the sorcerers, the idolaters, and all liars shall have their portion in the lake which burns with fire and brimstone. This is the second death" (Rev. 21:8). So in heaven there will be no blasphemy, no rudeness, no shaking of the fist at God, no God-haters. All the former things are passed away.

There will be no teaching on worship. We will fall on our faces and worship. No one will be self-conscious in heaven. As Robert Murray McCheyne put it: we will love "with unsinning heart."[1] There will be no competition, no wandering thoughts, no conflicting ideas. We will worship by the Spirit perfectly.

There will be no speculation in heaven. "For now we see as through a glass, dimly," said Paul (1 Cor. 13:12). But then there will be no theological speculation, no eschatological speculation, no trying to project how it is going to turn out in the end. You won't worry, "What is God's will for me? Did I do this right? What is that other person thinking?" We won't want to know, "Did Paul write Hebrews? Was Matthew's the first Gospel?" Our small and large questions will be answered.

There will be no more sun in heaven. It is interesting that twice in the Book of Revelation we are told that there is no need of the sun. All things will be new there. There will be no thorns, no decay, no curse on the land, no earthquakes, no hurricanes. Heaven and earth will pass away. There will be no moon, no clouds, no worry about weather, no equator, no rotation of the earth around the sun, no change of seasons, no need for central heating, no nuclear energy, no worry about the ozone layer.

There will be no separation in heaven. When Paul addressed the church at Ephesus, he said, "Now I know that all you, among whom I went proclaiming the kingdom of God, will see my face no more" (Acts 20:25). After he had finished, they all knelt down on the shore just before Paul got on the boat and prayed. They all began to cry. They hugged and kissed him and they grieved because he had said that they wouldn't ever see him again. Most of us remember the grief we felt the last time we saw one of our loved ones or a close friend or a minister who was very special to us. No more sorrow like that. There will not even be tears for lost loved ones. I can't imagine how that will be. I can't understand how heaven can be a place of joy if any of my loved ones were in hell. But it says, "God shall wipe away all tears from their eyes" (Rev. 21:4).

There will be no sickness in heaven. "'There shall be no more death.' Neither shall there be any more sorrow nor crying nor pain, for the former things have passed away" (Rev. 21:4). No disease. Some people have migraines; others have arthritis and don't know what it is like to tie their shoes without pain; some have cancer or the agony of seeing their loved ones suffer with cancer. It's hard to imagine an existence without pain. There will be no handicapped people, no one with mental illness. "Look! I am making all things new."

What will there be in heaven? First, restoration. Have you noticed that little phrase in Acts 3:21: "until the times of restitution of all things" (KJV)? This means the restoration of what was lost in the Fall. What was lost in Eden will be restored, never to be threatened again. Hebrews 9:23 talks about the heavens being purified. One of the reasons for this is to make sure that there will never again be a revolt.

In heaven we will worship as Adam did before the Fall, with one big difference—we will have something to be thankful for that Adam was not aware of when he was created in the image of God. There was no sin in Adam before the Fall, so he worshipped without sin. But when we get to heaven, we will worship with hearts overflowing with gratitude, for we will worship with the knowledge that we are redeemed by the precious blood of Jesus. "And they sang a new song, saying: 'You are worthy to take the scroll, and to open its seals; for You were slain, and have redeemed us to God by Your blood out of every tribe and tongue and people and nation'" (Rev. 5:9).

John says, "He showed me a pure river of the water of life, clear as crystal" (Rev. 22:1). There will be a flowing river, a tree of life with fruit to be eaten. We will probably be eating and drinking in heaven because there will be no hunger, no thirst. There will be enough for everybody.

There will be fellowship—"a great multitude which no one could count" (Rev. 7:9). Even in man's unfallen state God said, "It is not good that the man should be alone" (Gen. 2:18). So in heaven there will be restoration of friendships. In our churches there are people who don't speak to each other. But there will be no way you can avoid someone by sitting on the other side of the new Jerusalem—nor will we want to. We will love the people that we feel uneasy with today.

There will be righteousness in heaven. That means transparent holiness and perfect justice. There will be no miscarriage of justice in heaven, whether by courts, elections, congressional hearings, or bribery. There will be no discrimination, no racial prejudice, no conspiracies, but total fairness. God looks forward to that. Do you think God doesn't care when somebody is kidnapped, mugged, or libeled? But He sees the end from the beginning. He never panics. He can wait for His name to be cleared.

There will be reunion in heaven. I shall see my mother again, my grandparents, my maternal grandfather who taught me to fish. Did you ever hear the song: "Will the circle be unbroken by and by, Lord, by and by?"[2] Those who were in the circle with us but are no longer here will be with us again. We will all be together in heaven. Do you know of some who are not saved now? Do you have a loved one who is not saved? Maybe you are the link in the circle between that person and heaven.

What will heaven be like? It will be revelation. The truth will be equally clear to all then. And best of all, Jesus will be fully revealed. "For now we see as through a glass, dimly, but then, face to face" (1 Cor. 13:12). We are all going to see Him. My Lord and my God. The One who died for me. The One who comes alongside in my darkest hour. The One I love.

There will be rejoicing in heaven. John said that he heard a loud voice, "'Worthy is the Lamb who was slain, to receive power and riches and wisdom and strength and honor and glory and blessing!' Then I heard every creature which is in heaven and on the earth and under the earth and in the sea, and all that are in them, saying: 'To Him who sits on the throne and to the Lamb be blessing and honor and glory and power, forever and ever!'" (Rev. 5:12–13). Rejoicing that will never end. Sometimes we experience moments of ecstasy or complete happiness. We say, "If only this could go on and on and on." What is so thrilling is that in heaven it will be like that.

When we've been there ten thousand years,
Bright shining as the sun,
We've no less days to sing God's praise
Than when we'd first begun.[3]

A million years later will be like the first day. We will discover—I guarantee it—that the joy of God alone is greater than any joy yet known to man. Greater joy than any physical or sensual or intellectual pleasure. Greater joy than any success or any vindication or any promotion.

And, finally, there will be reverence in heaven: "They sang the song of Moses, the servant of God, and the song of the Lamb, saying: 'Great and marvelous are Your works, Lord God Almighty! Just and true are Your ways, O King of saints! Who shall not fear You, O Lord, and glorify Your name? For You alone are holy" (Rev. 15:3–4). No intimacy with God, no knowledge of Him, will diminish the fear, the awesomeness, and the reverence we will feel.

I don't know all we will be doing in heaven. But I do know we will worship God and the Lord Jesus Christ without any sin and without any self-consciousness. We will worship spontaneously, by the Holy Spirit, without any limitation or hindrance whatever.

May God give us a taste of worship like this while we still have the opportunity to respond to the preached Word. We only have one life, and it will soon be past. And only what is done for Jesus—in love and worship and gratitude—will last.

NOTES

FOREWORD

1. Augustine, "Sermon 34," *The Works of Saint Augustine: A Translation for the 21st Century*, Part III-Sermons, vol. 11: Sermons 20–50, trans. Edmund Hill, ed. John E. Rotelle (Brooklyn, NY: New City Press, 1990), 168.

CHAPTER 1 | Spirit-Filled Worship

1. Blue Letter Bible, s.v. "*proskyneō*," accessed August 18, 2016, https://www.blueletterbible.org/lang/lexicon/lexicon .cfm?Strongs=G4352&t=KJV.
2. Blue Letter Bible, s.v. "*latreuō*," accessed August 18, 2016, https://www.blueletterbible.org/lang/lexicon/lexicon .cfm?Strongs=G3000&t=KJV.
3. A. W. Tozer, *Whatever Happened to Worship? A Call to True Worship* (Camp Hill, PA: WingSpread Publishers 2012).
4. Samuel Stennett, "Majestic Sweetness Sits Enthroned," public domain.
5. Martin Luther, "A Mighty Fortress Is Our God," trans. Fredrick H. Hedge, public domain.
6. Charles M. Fillmore, "Tell Mother I'll Be There," public domain.
7. A. W. Tozer, *Whatever Happened to Worship? A Call to True Worship* (Camp Hill, PA: WingSpread Publishers 2012).

CHAPTER 4 | Fellowship

1. Jonathan Edwards, "True Grace Distinguished From the Experience of Devils," in The Works of Jonathan Edwards, A.M., volume 2 (London: Ball, Arnold, and Co. 1840), 43.

CHAPTER 5 | Worship, Preaching, and the Preacher

1. Charles Spurgeon, as quoted in *Preaching and Preachers*, D. Martyn Lloyd-Jones (Grand Rapids, MI: Zondervan 2011), 118.

Chapter 6 | Worship and Listening

1. Alexander Maclaren, *Expositions of Holy Scripture*, Ephesians 1:19, accessed August 18, 2016, http://biblehub.com/commentaries/ephesians/1-19.htm.
2. William Cowper, "Sometimes a Light Surprises," public domain.

Chapter 8 | Worshipping in the Dark

1. Anonymous, "How Firm a Foundation," public domain.

Chapter 11 | Lifestyle Worship

1. Brother Lawrence, *The Practice of the Presence of God*, Christian Classics Ethereal Library, accessed August 19, 2016, http://www.ccel.org/ccel/lawrence/practice.iii.iv.html.

Chapter 14 | Learning From Angels

1. Robert Murray McCheyne, "When This Passing World Is Done," public domain.
2. Johnson Oatman, Jr., "Holy, Holy, Is What the Angels Sing," public domain.

Chapter 15 | Spiritual Warfare in Worship

1. Augustine, *City of God* (Harmondsworth, Middlesex, UK: Penguin, 1972), 22.1 (p. 1023).
2. John Newton, "Approach, My Soul, the Mercy Seat," public domain.
3. Charlotte Elliott, "Just As I Am, Without One Plea," public domain.

Chapter 16 | …With Giving

1. William Shakespeare, *Hamlet, Prince of Denmark*, Act III, Scene 2, Line 179.
2. J. B. Phillips, *The New Testament in Modern English*, Heading of 2 Corinthians 9:7–15, (New York: Touchstone 1995).

CHAPTER 20 | ...With the Whole Personality

1. William Shakespeare, *Hamlet, Prince of Denmark*, Act I, Scene 3, Line 78.

CHAPTER 23 | The Joy of Doing Nothing

1. John Calvin, *Selections From His Writings*, ed. John Dillenberger (Oxford, UK: Oxford University Press 1975), 401.
2. Charles Spurgeon, "Life More Abundant, No. 1150," January 4, 1874 at Metropolitan Tabernacle, accessed August 23, 2016, http://www.spurgeongems.org/vols19-21/chs1150.pdf.
3. Brother Lawrence, *The Practice of the Presence of God*, Christian Classics Ethereal Library, accessed August 23, 2016, http://www.ccel.org/ccel/lawrence/practice.iii.ii.html.

CHAPTER 24 | Worship and Revival

1. Voltaire, letter to Mme. d'Épinal, Ferney, December 26, 1760, accessed August 23, 2016, http://www.qotd.org/search/single.html?qid=34264.

CHAPTER 25 | Preparation for Ultimate Worship

1. Isaac Watts, "Alas! And Did My Savior Bleed," public domain.
2. Charles Wesley, "O for a Thousand Tongues to Sing," public domain.

CHAPTER 26 | Worship in Heaven

1. Robert Murray McCheyne, "When This Passing World Is Done," public domain.
2. Ada R. Habershon, "Will the Circle Be Unbroken?," public domain.
3. John Newton, "Amazing Grace," public domain.

CONNECT WITH US!

**CHARISMA
HOUSE**

(Spiritual Growth)

 Facebook.com/CharismaHouse

@CharismaHouse

Instagram.com/CharismaHouse

SILOAM

(Health)

Pinterest.com/CharismaHouse

**MODERN
ENGLISH
VERSION**

(Bible)
www.mevbible.com